MRS BEETON'S
HAND-MADE GIFTS

CONSULTANT EDITOR
Bridget Jones

WARD LOCK

A WARD LOCK BOOK

First published in 1995 by Ward Lock,
Wellington House,
125 Strand,
London
WC2R OBB

A Cassell Imprint
Copyright © Ward Lock 1995

Mrs Beeton's is a registered trademark of Ward Lock Ltd

Edited by Jenni Fleetwood
Designed by Ben Cracknell
Photography by Sue Atkinson
Home Economists Carol Handslip and Jacqui Hine
Knitting, Crochet and Embroidery by Ionne Hammond

British Library Cataloguing-in-Publication Data
A catalogue record of this book is available from the
British Library

ISBN 07063-73571-X

Printed in Spain

– Contents –

The Joy of Giving

The exchange of gifts is an ancient practice, as instinctive as it is cultural; the process of giving and receiving, together with all that it implies, is evident in the natural behaviour of some animals as well as in humans. The notion of giving and receiving has developed over centuries. In primitive societies gifts of appeasement were made to gods, rulers or people who held high office in the hope of approval and good fortune. Ancient ceremonies, many of which have evolved into the annual feasts and festivals we celebrate today, involved the making and exchanging of presents. Early travellers and explorers presented gifts to the people they met in foreign lands as tokens of goodwill and in the hope of acceptance, or at least to pre-empt any hostile reaction to their arrival. This custom survives today, but it has become a grand international gesture of peace and comradeship, and such institutional offerings are an accepted part of contemporary diplomacy. When visiting guests bring gifts they are maintaining the same tradition, but the gesture is much more personal. Gift giving today is an accepted way of expressing friendship and affection – or simply a way of saying thank you.

Celebrations and Special Occasions

Apart from impulse presents, surprises and love tokens, gifts tend to mark specific occasions, such as seasonal feasts or personal celebrations. In the past, rigid conventions applied, with certain gifts being deemed acceptable to mark such events as weddings, christenings or anniversaries, but the modern accent is on meeting individual needs and likes. It is often the most unconventional idea that gives the greatest pleasure. The gift which is opened to laughter and applause will always be remembered. This is what the joy of giving is all about: forethought, ideas and inspiration, not a feverish shopping expedition that lacks enthusiasm. When thought and attention are paid to the likes and dislikes, or sometimes to the practical everyday requirements, of the person for whom the present is planned, the most modest gesture can bring immeasurable pleasure to both the giver and the recipient. Home-made items are always valued and culinary treats are highly acceptable.

Annual Feasts

Seasonal celebrations have become commercial occasions, and the fun of preparing for them can be masked by the constant bombardment by retailers marketing their wares. This is not new, of course, and in Mrs Beeton's day *The Englishwoman's Domestic Magazine* carried its share of advertisements for gifts, especially for Valentine's day and Christmas. Shopping was a relatively simple exercise then, involving lists and expeditions, exchanges of ideas and the examination of goods over a counter. By comparison we are

left very much to our own devices in the modern, self-service shopping environment, and we seldom ask the advice of sales assistants when choosing gifts. So, as soon as it is remotely justifiable, stores display and advertise their seasonal stock. Take these first signs of the forthcoming festivities as your cue to begin planning home-made gifts and make the process a creative one rather than an annual chore.

New Year's Day

The tradition of first footing is still upheld in Scotland. Following the Hogmanay celebrations of New Year's Eve, a dark-haired man is invited to be the first person to enter the house after midnight. He brings with him gifts of coal (one lump suffices), salt and bread to bring good luck to the household for the rest of the year.

The traditional Welsh custom for New Year's Day was the collection of 'calenig'. The children of the community went out before noon and knocked on doors to wish their neighbours a Happy New Year. Sometimes they sang or recited seasonal rhymes, and there was always a reward of one penny or a suitable treat, such as a piece of cake. The custom has largely fallen into disuse.

Wassailing is another seasonal activity that has all but ceased. In the past a wassail bowl of hot punch was carried through the streets for all to sample and share. Scottish children, like their Welsh contemporaries, collected fruit – especially apples – and money. One wassail song was quite explicit:

> 'Wassail, wassail through the town,
> If you've got any apples,
> throw them down;
> If you've got no apples,
> money will do,
> If you've got no money,
> God bless you.'

Despite the fact that this custom is not common outside Scotland, New Year's Day is traditionally a popular time for celebrating with family or friends, and those who do not exchange Christmas cards or gifts often do so at the start of another year.

Valentine's Day

February 14th is the opportunity for shy would-be suitors to indicate their intentions to their prospective lovers – but not too clearly as it is the tradition for greetings and gifts to be made anonymously. The true origins of the occasion are questionable. Legend has it that St Valentine was the bishop of Terni, and he was martyred in Rome. February 14th was his feast day; however, this character no longer appears on the calendar of saints. St Valentine's day falls on the day before the Roman festival of Lupercalia, when sacrifices and celebrations were made to the gods from the cave in which Romulus and Remus, legendary twins and founders of Rome, were said to have been suckled by a wolf.

According to 'The Englishwoman in London' feature in one issue of The Englishwoman's Domestic Magazine, part of the pagan festivities of Lupercalia involved men drawing the names of certain young women from a box, a custom that became outmoded when the celibacy of priests was introduced. The result was that 'jealousy of the festival, and envy, naturally enough, arose in the minds of men who were denied alike the blessings of a reciprocal affection and the comforts of a home'. The priests tried to eradicate the practice by substituting the names of particular saints for those of the women and the celebrations were moved to Saint Valentine's anniversary. Their attempts were unsuccessful as the choosing of valentines was not quashed, on the contrary it spread abroad.

'For many years, even among the nobility, it was the custom in this country to draw lots, which were termed valentines, on the eve before St. Valentine's Day. The names of a select number of one sex were, by an equal number of the other sex, put into a vessel, and, as the different names were drawn, it was looked upon as a good omen of their being man and wife afterwards. It was practised by the gentry as early as 1476, and deemed obsolete in that class about 1645.'

The custom gradually became a joke practised by married couples, both men and women, as well as bachelors and spinsters. Mottoes were drawn along with the names, and hand-lettered greetings and light-hearted rhymes were sent to valentines. Elaborate or expensive gifts were sent to ladies, as when 'half-a-dozen pairs of gloves and a pair of silk stockings and garters' were dispatched by a Sir W. Batten to Mr Pepys' wife.

By Mrs Beeton's era, the festivities were once again based on match-making, and although Valentine's day provided an opportunity for jokes that were sometimes unkind, on the whole it was an occasion when young ladies received tokens from their admirers, some extremely light-hearted and others more intense. The day had expanded into something of a season for 'juvenile lovers'. Stationers had started to cash in on the popularity of the occasion, producing amazing Victorian Valentine's cards adorned with cherubs, hearts, roses and lace. From the penny valentine to extravagant purchases, the feature noted that 'the depth of the purse is not equal to the depth of the affection.'

Mothering Sunday

Mothering Sunday (or Mother's Day) falls on the fourth Sunday in Lent in the United Kingdom, the second Sunday in Lent in Australia and America. This is a comparatively modern festival which evolved – according to one explanation – when young girls were sent into service. The girls worked hard in the great houses and had little spare time, so they were given time off and sent home to see their families on this one Sunday in the year.

This has always been one of the more homely festivals, when children treat their mothers to breakfast in bed, offer to wash the dishes or perform some other loving service. In the spirit of the occasion, children like to make cards for their

mothers and may prepare a hand-made gift, bake a cake or make some biscuits when they are old enough. Although there is a wide selection of commercial cards and presents available, there is nothing to match a small token of affection made with care and determination by a young child.

Easter

Throughout the Christian world, Easter is the main holiday of the year along with Christmas. Eggs, a symbol of new life, are dyed in coloured water, then served as a colourful breakfast. Fresh eggs are blown and the empty shells painted to create lasting gifts. Chocolate eggs come in all shapes and sizes, and, of course, they can be made at home. An Easter egg hunt is the traditional activity for entertaining children. Chocolate eggs are hidden around the garden, or through the house in poor weather, and the children race to find them. The eggs

may be labelled with the names of the children to ensure that everyone gets his or her fair share.

At one time Easter parades were popular, when ladies would wear new bonnets decorated with spring flowers and ribbons. Later, hats replaced the bonnets and today the custom is commemorated in competitions to trim the best bonnet at the

Easter fair. Other customs still commemorated in some communities include the distribution of buns to the young and old, or traditionally to the poor and needy of the parish. Egg rolling competitions and egg and spoon races are also popular at Easter fairs. In some small seafaring communities, this may be a time when the fishing nets are blessed in preparation for the summer season.

Spring flowers are the classic alternative gift to chocolate eggs. A batch of freshly baked hot cross buns, some Easter biscuits or a simnel cake are all equally acceptable.

Father's Day
A modern custom, said to be American in origin, Father's Day started in the early part of this century. It is celebrated on the third Sunday in June. Being a more recent innovation than Mother's Day, this tends to be more commercial, but it is still an excellent opportunity for children to paint cards or make small gifts.

Halloween
On the last day of October, on the eve of All Saints Day, the custom was for children to dress up as witches or fiends and call on neighbours or friends asking for a 'trick or treat'. The idea is to offer the young jokers gifts of sweets, apples, money or some other suitable treat to prevent them from playing a trick.

Christmas
The main feast of the Christian year and the one for which the most preparation is made. The activities focus on the religious festival and this is very much a time for rejoicing. The celebrations lead up to the two-day holiday and often continue through to the new year. Houses are decorated, friends and family gather to exchange cards and presents and enjoy traditional foods.

Despite the vast commercial value of the season, and the fact that we cannot escape the economic significance of this, many still take pride in making their own cards and creating simple, thoughtful gifts as well as concentrating their energies on traditional preserving and cooking.

Family Occasions

Engagement
The ring presented to his bride by the groom-to-be is the outward sign that a couple intend to marry. Engagement gifts are usually given by close friends and relatives, so they tend to be chosen carefully to reflect either the taste of the couple or their specific practical requirements. This may be a suitable occasion for giving something for that old-fashioned 'bottom drawer'.

Weddings
When young people lived with their parents until they married, wedding presents were intended to set them up in their new homes. Today, many people have established their independence well before marriage. The change is often from being a single person renting in a bedsit or sharing a flat to buying property, so practical considerations are still important in many cases. However, there is an increasing trend towards later marriage, well after a home has been established, so the focus has shifted to luxury gifts.

The bride and groom exchange wedding rings and they may well give each other small gifts. They will also give small, lasting, tokens of the occasion to bridesmaids and attendants. Some couples also present their mothers with small commemorative items, and the guests may also be given simple gifts, known as favours. These are usually sugared almonds, decoratively wrapped in lace and ribbon.

The fashion for preparing a wedding present list has evolved. This is a comprehensive list of the requirements for the couple's home, detailing colour schemes and with some general ideas for presents as well as precise details of crockery, glassware and other pieces that the couple intend to collect. The list, which should include items in a range of prices, is distributed by the bride or her mother to those who request it. Larger shops and some chain stores provide a wedding list service, and this is favoured by many as it allows friends to browse through the list and make a choice without any embarrassment on either side. This method also has the advantage of being well organised as gifts are less likely to be duplicated.

Births

The birth of a baby or the christening are occasions for genuine once-only gifts. Silver is the traditional choice, with egg cups and spoons, charms and/or bracelets, silver chains and tankards being popular presents. Since silver can be expensive, and because slavishly sticking to tradition can result in the baby receiving many identical presents, items of clothing and toys are often bought. Money intended for a savings account is another practical choice. Selecting something that can be kept until the child grows up is a good idea and small pieces of glass crystal or fine china can be most acceptable, but it is wise to avoid large items which will clutter up the family home or which are likely to be displayed and damaged well before the child is a teenager.

Wedding Anniversaries

Although some couples mark each wedding anniversary with a celebration, it is customary for friends and relatives to acknowledge silver, ruby and golden anniversaries with greetings and gifts.

Birthdays

The celebration of adult birthdays is quite personal. Many people prefer not to mark their increasing age other than by some simple family acknowledgement. In the past it was traditional for ladies, in particular, to keep their ages a secret.

However, most people look forward to the opportunity of sharing a special meal with family or friends and enjoy opening presents. The presents themselves, for the majority of birthdays, are normally thoughtful or clever rather than extravagant. Home-made gifts are the ideal choice for children to give their parents, and food items are especially suitable for giving to friends, when an informal acknowledgement of the occasion is all that is required.

Coming of age is the traditional rite of passage for young people. This was when the key of the door was handed over as a sign of independence and trust. The person was also considered to be sufficiently responsible to take an active part in more serious aspects of society. Originally this took place on the 21st birthday, but the coming of age has since been moved down to 18 years. This is when the right to vote is given and when the individual takes legal responsibilities. The 18th birthday has become the more significant date, but many people also celebrate their 21st birthday with a family celebration, if not with a large party.

Birth Signs, Stones and Flowers

The belief in astrological influences at the time of birth is an ancient one, and even sceptics take a light-hearted interest in the subject. The following list shows the signs of the zodiac according to the date and month of an individual's birth. Certain gemstones and flowers are associated with each of the birth signs, or sometimes with different months of the year, and these are meant to bring good luck to those whose birthdays they represent. Astrology is a complex subject which is studied in depth; the following is simply a list of signs that may be of interest or of value when thinking up ideas for suitable birthday gifts.

WEDDING ANNIVERSARIES YEAR BY YEAR

1	2	3	4	5	6	7	8	9	10	11	12
paper	cotton	leather	linen	wood	iron	wool	bronze	pottery	tin	steel	silk
13	14	15	20	25	30	35	40	45	50	55	60
lace	ivory	crystal	china	silver	pearl	jade	ruby	sapphire	gold	emerald	diamond

- The Art of Giving -

Presents may be packed in a variety of different styles. The decoration can be simple or elaborate, functional or artistic, pretty or dramatic – it takes ideas, enthusiasm and time to transform simple materials into spectacular results. Crisp, neat wrapping can be finished with a sharp band of ribbon or softer paper may be pleated and then topped with a lavish bow; plain wrappers can be decorated with ribbon streamers or a plain-coloured box made glamorous by sticking on golden stars. For best results, allow time for packing and adding the finishing touches, and plan ahead to make sure you have all the materials required.

Difficult Shapes and Sizes

An oblong box with neat corners is the easiest shape to pack and decorate; unfortunately, few gifts fit that description. One solution is to pack the item in a box before wrapping it. When you have a soft, rather shapeless, but quite special, item to pack, it is a good idea to wrap it in tissue and tie it with baby ribbon before packing it in a box bought especially for the purpose. The fun of receiving such a glorious package emphasises the beauty of a delicate gift like a silk scarf, gloves or lightweight clothing.

Save empty boxes for less-glamorous presents or pick them up in supermarkets. A plastic carton originally used for mushrooms or similar vegetables will often provide a sufficiently firm base for neat packing or it may be covered with colourful paper and the gift loosely wrapped in crepe or tissue paper, then placed on the carton or tray and tied with ribbon. Empty cereal packets can also be salvaged and cut down if necessary to be used as containers. Most people will appreciate the humour in unwrapping a splendid package only to find a cereal packet inside, or the packet can be disguised by spraying it with coloured paint or silver or gold spray.

Bottles and jars are extremely difficult, not only because of their shape but also because they break easily. Tall slim carrier bags sold specifically for wine are useful and they also alert the recipient to take care when handling the present. If you do use ordinary wrapping, it should be pleated neatly around the base of the bottle, taped firmly in place up the side, then pleated in and taped at the top. Alternatively, use a soft crepe paper, gathering it into small pleats around the neck of the bottle. Having taped it in place, trim the excess to leave the top of the bottle exposed. Neaten the top of the paper with a band of ribbon and add an voluptuous bow with tails or ringlets of ribbon. This is fun when the bottle has an attractive top, such as a champagne clasp or an interesting stopper as are sometimes used on bottles of olive oil.

Round packs are equally irritating – you can spend ages trying to wrap a tin of biscuits or a cake tin, smoothing, folding and pressing paper into place only to find that the package looks as though it was cobbled together in a few seconds, despite all your efforts and the hundreds of bits of discreetly placed sticky tape. One solution is to wrap the gift, then neaten the side with a deep band of smooth paper (rather like a cake frill). This only works with the right choice of paper; it should be supple enough to conform to the shape of the package, but firm enough to give a crisp outline. Another

Fresh and dried flowers or growing herbs make excellent gifts: a wire basket for mounting on a wall can be decorated with ribbon and filled with dried flowers; a basket of culinary herbs will delight gardeners or gourmets; and inexpensive plastic pots can be quickly transformed by gluing on a binding of twine or decorative string.

answer might be to cover the object with soft crepe paper, then wrap a wide, folded band of crisp paper around the side. Make a feature of the join in the paper as the front of the gift by gluing folds of paper or ribbon over it.

A flamboyant and free approach can work well instead of trying to force the package to take a regimented shape. Thick paper is not suitable in this case and crepe is usually too floppy, so try tissue, and lots of it. Swathe the tissue around the gift, taping it in place here and there, allowing corners to protrude at odd angles and gathering the wrapping in towards the top of the package. Rosettes or ribbon streamers, or even paper party decorations, will distract attention from any deficiencies in neatness. The edges of the paper may be sprayed with gold, silver or a contrasting colour.

The other option for awkward angles is to drape a wrapping over them from the top. First cover the present as best you can with paper – a single-coloured sheet can be a good choice. The drape should flow from the top of the gift down the sides to disguise creases in the underwrapping without covering it completely. Tissue is useful as it allows the colour of the under paper to show through. Crepe does not drape well over wide shapes, but it will work when adding a short 'frill' over the top of a slim item. A drape can also be made from moderately soft or thin wrapping paper cut into narrow strips. Alternatively, a curtain of fine ribbon can be glued on the top of the gift, with the pieces overlapped or doubled as necessary to achieve the required result.

Perishables

It is important to consider the practicalities of ensuring that perishables stay fresh and advising the recipient to keep the present chilled. Think about the choice of food gift carefully and avoid giving something which has to be eaten within a day or two when the person is likely to have a well-stocked refrigerator. For example, a dish of soused herrings may be a birthday treat for someone who lives alone but they are unlikely to be as welcome over the Christmas season when there are plenty of other perishable foods which need eating up quickly. Foods which do not keep well should be prepared just before they are given; on the same day or the day before at the most. Savoury home-cooked items are especially welcomed by elderly persons living alone but it is important to emphasise that the gift must be chilled (if necessary) and eaten within one or two days.

Rather than wrapping an item in paper and running the risk of disguising the fact that it is food, it is often best to pack the food neatly in a serving dish, attractive container, basket or jar. Cover it tightly with cling film, if necessary, or wrap it neatly and securely in a polythene bag. Then add a decoration of ribbon and a tag with storage instructions and 'eat-by' information. It can also be useful to add serving suggestions.

All this information means that the tag has to be larger than usual, so buy an attractive postcard or a small folded card and punch a hole in it, then attach it with a thin ribbon. Used Christmas cards can be successfully recycled for this purpose. Alternatively cut out a large novelty tag from thin card.

Sending or Posting

Choosing a present that is highly perishable or particularly fragile, spending time and effort (and money!) applying secure packing, then worrying about it every minute until it is opened and – hopefully – its safety is confirmed is really not worth the anguish. When relying on the mail, avoid making or buying anything which is exceptionally fragile or (unless you want to invest a small fortune in carriage) heavy.

The decorative wrapping should be restrained and fairly flat otherwise it will be squashed beyond recognition when an outer covering is applied. Plastic bubble wrap or padded envelopes should be used. If necessary, the item can be placed in a cardboard box and surrounded by bubble wrap or paper – old wallpaper is useful, but avoid newspaper as the ink tends to come off, making it unpleasantly messy. Use heavy-duty brown parcel tape to seal a box or envelope. Wrap thick brown parcel paper around a box and tape it in place. If the item is quite heavy, tying string around it will not only prevent the weight of the contents from damaging the wrapping, but it will also give handlers something to carry it by, limiting the likelihood of the corners becoming torn or damaged.

In addition to first or second class post and parcel post, items can be recorded, registered or sent by special delivery. Depending on the service, the item may be insured for a modest amount. Ask at the post office for details of different services and the cost, which is an extra charge added to the cost of posting the item. The railway also offers a delivery service between stations or, in some cases, delivered to the door; look for information about parcel services at your local station. National and international courier services are another option. Check your local telephone directories for companies operating in your area and enquire about their terms and charges.

Seasonal Decorations

Make use of seasonal materials or themes when packing gifts. For Christmas, use commercial decorations, such as tinsel and baubles, as well as holly, ivy and other evergreens in miniature arrangements. Most of the ideas that follow can be adapted for a variety of occasions, including birthdays and anniversaries.

Easter Egg Nest

Decorate the corner of a gift with a small nest of shredded tissue filled with miniature chocolate eggs. Cut out a plain tag from thick coloured paper or watercolour paper. Use yellow paint (watercolour or gouache) to tint the edge of a thick white tag yellow. Write a message on the tag. Wrap the gift in plain paper and glue the tag in place at an angle near one corner. Apply a small circle of glue to cover the stuck-down corner of the tag and some of the paper. Finely shred some green and yellow tissue (or use bought shredded tissue), mix both colours and stick them in a nest shape on the glue. Glue foil-wrapped mini chocolate eggs in the middle of the nest. Glue an Easter chick beside the nest.

Spray of Crystallised Flowers

This decoration is not edible. Pick small, perfect seasonal flowers and leaves, such as primroses, violets or rosebuds. Make sure they are clean and dry. Lightly whisk an egg white with a few drops of water so that it can be brushed easily. Brush the egg white over the flowers, then sprinkle them with caster sugar. Brush and sprinkle the leaves in the same way and leave both flowers and leaves on a wire rack until the sugar and egg white coating is crisp. Place small pieces of crumpled foil under one side of some flowers so that the petals dry in a raised position.

Make small loops of fine white, yellow and green gift ribbon or baby ribbon by cutting short lengths (about 5 cm/2 inches) and gluing their ends together. Leave the loops until the glue is dry. Write a message on a gift tag and stick it on the

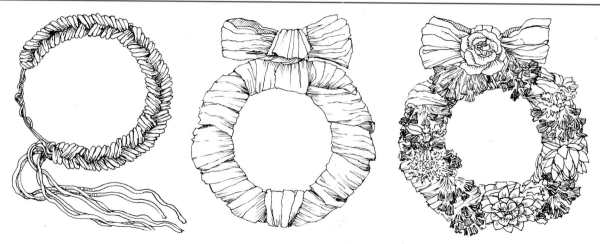

present, allowing room for an oval spray of flowers. Glue the flowers and leaves, working from the corner of the tag and curving them in an oval spray. Stick some flowers and ribbon loops to form the outline of the spray first, placing two or three small leaves towards the base of the spray. Then fill in the middle with more flowers and ribbon loops. The ribbon loops give height and support the flowers.

Miniature Flower Wreath

This can be used for all seasons, according to the choice of flowers which may be dried, silk or made from feathers.

Make a base for the wreath from macrame string, twisted paper or coarse twine and plastic-covered garden wire. Shape a ring of wire about 7.5 cm/ 3 inches in diameter and add a second circle, twisting the ends of the wire to make a reasonably firm ring. Small pointed pliers are useful for twisting the wire neatly and firmly. Bind and plait three pieces of string around the wire, tying the ends off neatly underneath or sticking them in place. Twist a short piece of wire into a loop above the ends of the plait. Tie a piece of ribbon or decorative string through the loop so that the finished wreath can be tied to the parcel. Thread a length of ribbon through the wire loop and tie it in a neat bow. It is

The Refreshing Foot Bath mixture (page 121) can be tied in colourful bundles or packed loose in an attractive box; a Drawstring Toilet Bag (page 119) can be filled with luxury soaps; and plain wrapping paper or tissue can be sprayed with a shell pattern (right), and the gilded shells used to decorate the top of the gift.

easier to add the string and bow before covering the wreath with flowers.

Using a darning needle and buff-coloured cotton, stitch silk or feather flowers and leaves into the string plait. If using dried flowers, glue them on to the string base with small bulbs of strong adhesive. Water-based glue is not suitable. Leave the glue to set.

Place a band of ribbon around the gift. Tie a tag to the fine ribbon or string on the wreath, then tie the wreath and tag together around the ribbon on the gift.

Gilded Shells

Ordinary seashells look quite special when sprayed gold. Shell arrangements can look clumsy when too many shells are used or when several different types of shell are glued together, but a simple shell theme can look stunning on a summertime gift, especially when you start with a unique paper design.

You will need some well-shaped shells, such as cockles, and a sheet of coloured paper. Tissue paper can be sprayed with a pattern and used as a lining for gift boxes (opposite) or to wrap a delicate or lightweight gift. Arrange the shells at random on the paper, placing them flat-side down. If you do not have enough shells to complete the sheet of paper, work on a small area at a time or spray a pattern at one end of

the paper to make a border. To achieve a neat shell design, spray the shells gold, until their rims and the paper immediately surrounding them is well coloured. Do not spray all of the paper, but leave the spaces between the shells lightly flecked with gold. Leave the shells on the paper until the paint has dried. Lift the shells off, place them on newspaper and finish spraying them. Use the coloured paper with the gold shell outlines to wrap the gift neatly.

Draw lengths of fine gold and blue gift ribbon across the blade of a pair of scissors until they curl (see page 20). Glue the ribbon on the present, placing the ends neatly together so that the curls fan out slightly. Arrange gilded shells around the top of the streamers, gluing them in place when you are happy with the design. Then attach another shell to conceal the ends of the ribbon. Tiny shells may be glued at random radiating from the main arrangement. Cut out a shell-shaped gift tag and spray the edge with gold paint.

Summer Swag

Pressed daisies are attractive on a summer present, while other pressed or preserved flowers can be arranged in a swag decoration. Cover the gift with plain paper – shiny blue paper works well under daisies. Cut a sheet of paper to the same size as the top of the present and draw scallops in position for the swag.

To make a daisy chain, pick large flowers and make a small slit in the stem of each, just below the flower head. Thread the stem of one daisy through the slit in the stem of another until the flowers are close and linked by a short length of stem. Build up the chain by threading daisies on to the stems of the flowers. Hold the chain against the drawing of scallops on the paper to check the length. Make sure that there are plenty of daisies along each swag but that the point at the top of

each has only a stem. If the swags are long, make separate chains for each one.

Carefully press the daisies in position on the drawing of the swag, pressing each flower neatly, and cover it with a piece of white blotting paper. Cover with a heavy book and leave for 2–3 days. Glue the daisy chain in place on the present, applying a tiny dab of glue under each flower head. Leave until completely dry.

Add small bows of ribbon at the ends of the swag and at the top of each point between the scallops. Make ribbon curls by drawing lengths of ribbon over the blade of a pair of scissors (see page 20); attach them under the bows.

Alternatively, simply glue artificial daisies into a swag, adding small leaves or short lengths of ribbon.

A selection of ideas for gifts and wrappings, including a Drawstring Make-up Bag and Covered Coat Hanger (both on page 119); simple cards and tags (page 20); gilded leaves and a spice-wreath decoration (both on page 18) and an ivy-leaf border sprayed on tissue paper.

Autumn Leaves

Use a leaf as a stencil for spraying a design on plain paper, using gold or a contrasting coloured paint.

Select richly coloured leaves for the arrangement and press them flat between two pieces of absorbent kitchen paper under a heavy book. Twist a length of fine floristry wire around the stalk end of each leaf, taking care not to break the leaf, then brush them with varnish or spray them with gold paint. Leave to dry.

The arrangement will depend on the type of leaf. Beech leaves are versatile and can be wired into a spray. Tie the ends of the wire with a bow of ribbon and trim excess wire with cutters.

Leaves can be used flat, instead of wired. They may be glued in a rosette arrangement or overlapped to form a border on top of the present. They can also be attached around the side of a gift, either straight on the wrapping paper or on a band of wide ribbon.

Acorns and Oak Leaves

Use an oak leaf as a stencil for spraying a pattern on plain paper. Spray two or three leaves and a few acorns gold, then leave to dry. Glue the leaves on the gift, overlapping them and bringing their stalk ends together.

Cut several lengths of narrow ribbon in autumn colours and glue them into loops. When dry, make an arrangement of loops and acorns at the base of the leaves, then, when you are happy with the arrangement, remove the acorns and stick the loops in place, then glue the acorns on top.

Spice and Herb Decorations

Whole spices make attractive arrangements, miniature swags and wreaths. Star anise, cinnamon sticks, blades of mace and chillies can all be sprayed with gold or silver and wired or glued together in an interesting pattern. Cinnamon stick bundles also look good with sprigs of bay leaves.

Fresh red and green chillies can be threaded on gold string or fine ribbon (use a darning needle to make holes through the tops of the chillies at the stalk ends) and tied together on a band of ribbon.

Star anise, chillies and bay leaves can all be used as templates for spraying a pattern on to plain coloured paper.

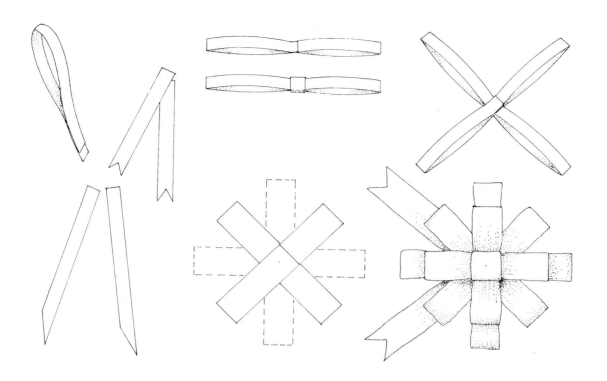

Ribbon Ideas

Gift wrapping ribbon is inexpensive and versatile but there are alternatives, such as floristry ribbon or ribbons made from all sorts of fabrics, such as silk, satin, velvet or gilded material. Wired ribbon has fine wire sewn into the edge of the fabric, allowing it to be twisted and shaped into beautiful bows, loops and tails. Gathered ribbons are also available to make full rosettes when the gathering thread is pulled.

Loops and Tails Cut lengths of ribbon and fold them in half to make loops. Trim the ends of short lengths at a slant or in a 'V' shape. Glue separate tails or loops of gift wrapping and floristry ribbon in position for best results.

Hoops Glue or tape lengths of gift wrapping or floristry ribbon into hoops and glue them on top of a present to make an unusual and stylish trimming.

Double cards are very effective: for instructions see page 20.

Neat Bows It is best to make a bow from separate pieces when using gift wrapping or floristry ribbon. Make a large double-ended loop of ribbon, gluing both ends underneath. Wrap a band of ribbon around the middle and attach short tails on the back.

Ribbon Curls To make gift wrapping or floristry ribbon curl, draw it sharply across one blade of a pair of scissors.

Ribbon Rosettes To make rosettes, make a series of double-ended loops of ribbon, starting with two large ones for the base and then reducing the size of the loops. Glue the first loops on top of each other in a cross, then add successive pairs of loops alternating their positions above the base pair. Double-sided adhesive tape is useful for sticking the loops on top of each other. Finish the rosette by sticking a small loop of ribbon in the middle.

Simple Cards and Tags

Simple home-made cards and tags complete the individual approach to present-giving. Children love making cards and they can achieve charming results with the most basic materials; coloured craft paper, crayons, paints, glitter and glue. However, adult interpretations of children's naïve art are seldom successful, so unless you have a genuine talent for drawing or painting it is better to adopt a more restrained approach by using good-quality materials with stylish, minimal decorations. You will find the materials and equipment you need in any good art shop. Ribbons, sequins and braids are available from the haberdashery departments of large stores or dressmaking shops.

✄ Use water colour papers, either white or tinted, hand-laid papers or other fine-quality papers and cards.

✄ Making a double card by using a flimsy paper as lining for a thick paper or card exterior is most effective. Use a fine pen to write a simple message on the flimsy paper.

✄ Make small cards which will stand easily and require only a minimal amount of decoration rather than large cards that take a lot of thought and attention.

✄ Gather all the materials and work out the design using a piece of scrap paper cut to size before cutting and gluing decorations on the card.

✄ Use a metal ruler and a scalpel to cut clean edges in one stroke. Use a clean chopping board as a base or work on a piece of thick cardboard.

✄ Mark the fold line down the middle of the card using a fine, light pencil, then lightly score the inside of thick card or paper.

✄ Attach the decoration to the front of the card and allow it to dry completely before folding the card down the scored or pencilled line.

✄ Cut an inner lining of lightweight or flimsy paper slightly smaller than the outer card and glue it in place with a dot or two of glue. Glue fine ribbon inside the card, applying three tiny dots of glue into the fold, then tie it in a neat bow halfway down the folded edge of the card on the outside.

Tissue can be gathered into a flamboyant bundle around an unevenly shaped gift and sprayed with gold or silver; plain boxes can be covered with wrapping paper; and evergreens or gilded cones are ideal decorations for Christmas packages.

— A Gift to Savour —

A Sample of Seafood

Salmon, prawns and shrimps, traditionally regarded as treats, are ideal ingredients for savoury gifts, such as pâtés and spreads. Pickled salmon or soused fish are more adventurous presents, likely to be greeted with delight by those who appreciate the preparation involved. All seafood gifts should be made on the day, or at most the day before, they are presented and the recipients advised that the food should be refrigerated and eaten promptly.

POTTED SALMON
Illustrated opposite

450 g/1 lb cold cooked salmon, skinned and boned
salt and pepper
pinch of cayenne pepper
pinch of ground mace
anchovy essence
50 g/2 oz softened clarified butter (page 25), plus
extra for sealing

Pound the salmon flesh in a mortar or process roughly in a blender or food processor. Add salt, pepper, cayenne, mace and anchovy essence to taste. Blend in the softened clarified butter thoroughly.

Rub the mixture through a fine sieve into a bowl. Turn into small pots. Cover with a layer of clarified butter and refrigerate until the butter is firm.

MAKES ABOUT 450 G/1 LB

POTTED SHRIMPS OR PRAWNS

225 g/8 oz unsalted butter
450 g/1 lb peeled cooked
shrimps or prawns
1.25 ml/¼ tsp ground white pepper
1.25 ml/¼ tsp ground mace
1.25 ml/¼ tsp ground cloves
dill sprigs to garnish

Melt the butter in a saucepan, add the shrimps or prawns and heat very gently, without boiling. Add the pepper, mace and cloves.

Using a slotted spoon, transfer the shrimps or prawns to small pots. Pour a little of the hot spiced butter into each pot.

Set the remaining spiced butter aside until the residue has settled, then pour over the shrimps or prawns. Chill until the butter is firm. Garnish with dill.

MAKES ABOUT 675 G/1½ LB

MRS BEETON'S TIP

Look out for small brown shrimps, sold in their shells, particularly in good fishmongers or coastal towns.

They have an excellent flavour which warrants the time and effort of peeling them. Buy double the quantity to allow for shell wastage.

A selection of savoury gifts: Raspberry Vinegar (page 33), Hot Reading Sauce (page 31), Potted Salmon, Herb Butter (page 35), Caraway Crackers (page 59) and Oatcakes (page 57).

HERRING ROE PATE

···

100 g/4 oz soft herring roes
salt and pepper
75 g/3 oz butter
30 ml/2 tbsp lemon juice
15 ml/1 tbsp chopped parsley

Sprinkle the herring roes with salt and pepper. Melt 25 g/1 oz of the butter in a small frying pan, add the roes and fry gently for 10 minutes. Process the roes to a smooth paste in a blender or food processor, or pound them in a mortar.

Soften the remaining butter and add it to the roe mixture, with the lemon juice and parsley. Turn into a small mould, cover and chill for 2 hours until set. Add a tag stressing that the pâté must be refrigerated and eaten within 48 hours. Add the following serving suggestion, if you wish. To serve, turn the pâté out of the mould, garnish with chopped lettuce and enjoy with fingers of hot dry toast or fresh brown bread.

MAKES ABOUT 175 G/6 OZ

SOUSED HERRINGS

···

6 herrings, scaled, heads and tails removed, and boned
salt and pepper
150 ml/¼ pint malt vinegar
15 ml/1 tbsp pickling spice
4 bay leaves
2 small onions, sliced in rings

Set the oven at 150°C/300°F/gas 2. Season the herrings with salt and pepper. Roll up the fillets, skin side in, from the tail end. Place neatly and fairly close together in an ovenproof baking dish.

In a jug, mix the vinegar with 100 ml/3½ fl oz water. Pour over the herrings, sprinkle with pickling spice and add the bay leaves. Lay the onion rings on top. Cover the fish loosely with foil and bake for 1½ hours. Remove from the oven and leave to cool completely. Using a slotted spoon, carefully transfer the rolls to a suitable container. Pour over the cooking liquid and spices, cover tightly and refrigerate until ready to present.

SERVES 6

GRAVAD LAX

···

Gravad Lax is a super gift to take when visiting friends for the weekend. Marinate the salmon for 24–48 hours and pack it in a suitable container with the marinating juices. It will keep for another 1–3 days, and will not disrupt any culinary plans your host or hostess have already made. Write out the instructions for turning and serving the fish on an attractive postcard, and tie it around the outside of the container. Pack the sauce in a separate airtight jar.

----

2 pieces unskinned salmon fillet,
total weight about 1 kg/2¼ lb, scaled
200 g/7 oz salt
90 g/3½ oz caster sugar
50 g/2 oz white peppercorns, crushed
90 g/3½ oz fresh dill, plus extra to garnish

MUSTARD SAUCE
30 ml/2 tbsp Swedish mustard (or other mild mustard)
10 ml/2 tsp caster sugar
15 ml/1 tbsp chopped fresh dill
45–60 ml/3–4 tbsp sunflower oil
lemon juice to taste
salt and pepper

Score the skin on each salmon fillet in 4 places. Mix the salt, sugar and peppercorns in a bowl.

Sprinkle a third of the salt mixture on the base of a shallow dish. Place one salmon fillet, skin side down, on the mixture. Cover with a further third of the salt mixture and add half the dill. Arrange the second fillet, skin side up, on top. Cover with the remaining salt mixture and dill.

Cover with foil. Place a plate or oblong baking sheet or tin on top of the fish and weight it down. Leave in the refrigerator for 36 hours, during which time the salt mixture will become a brine solution. Turn the whole fillet 'sandwich' every day and baste with the liquor.

For the sauce, mix the mustard, sugar and dill. Add the oil very slowly, beating all the time to make a thick sauce. Stir in a little lemon juice with salt and pepper to taste.

Drain off the brine, scape away the dill and peppercorns before serving. Serve thinly sliced, garnished with fresh dill, with the mustard sauce.

SERVES 4 TO 6

Pâtés and Potted Meats

These classic Christmas gifts are also a good choice of present when visiting, especially for male friends who may not swoon over creamy chocolates. And for friends who are moving into a new home, why not buy an attractive pot or a useful terrine and fill it with one of these savoury recipes?

POTTED HAM

butter for greasing
1.25 kg/2¾ lb cooked ham,
not too lean
1.25 ml/¼ tsp ground mace
1.25 ml/¼ tsp grated nutmeg
pinch of cayenne pepper
1.25 ml/¼ tsp ground black pepper
melted clarified butter (see Mrs Beeton's Tip)

Grease a pie dish. Set the oven at 180°C/350°F/gas 4. Mince the ham two or three times, then pound well and rub through a fine sieve into a clean bowl. Add the spices and seasonings; mix well. Spoon the ham mixture into the prepared dish, cover with buttered greaseproof paper and bake for about 45 minutes.

When cooked, allow to cool, then turn into small pots and cover with clarified butter. Refrigerate until the butter is firm.

MAKES ABOUT 1 KG/2¼ LB

MRS BEETON'S TIP

To clarify butter, heat gently until melted, then stand for 2–3 minutes. Carefully pour the clear yellow liquid on top into a clean bowl, leaving the residue behind. This is the clarified butter.

POTTED VENISON

100–150 g/4–5 oz butter
1 kg/2¼ lb cooked venison, finely minced
60 ml/4 tbsp port or brown stock
1.25 ml/¼ tsp grated nutmeg
1.25 ml/¼ tsp ground allspice
salt
2.5 ml/½ tsp freshly ground black pepper
melted clarified butter (see Mrs Beeton's Tip)

Melt 100 g/4 oz of the butter in a saucepan. Add the minced venison, port or stock, spices, salt and pepper. If the meat is very dry, add the remaining butter.

Cook the mixture gently until blended and thoroughly hot. Immediately, turn into small pots and leave to cool. Cover with clarified butter. When cold, refrigerate until the butter is firm.

MAKES ABOUT 1 KG/2¼ LB

POTTED GAME

350 g/12 oz cooked boneless game meat, trimmed
100 g/4 oz cooked ham or boiled bacon, trimmed
75 g/3 oz butter, softened
pinch of cayenne pepper
salt
1.25 ml/¼ tsp ground black pepper
melted clarified butter (see Mrs Beeton's Tip)

GARNISH
bay leaves
juniper berries

Mince the game and ham or bacon very finely. Pound it to a smooth paste, gradually working in the butter. Alternatively, grind the meats in a food processor; add the butter and process briefly to combine. Mix in the cayenne, with salt and pepper to taste.

Turn the mixture into small pots and cover with clarified butter. Garnish with bay leaves and juniper berries. Refrigerate the pots until the butter is firm.

MAKES ABOUT 450 G/1 LB

POTTED BEEF

A popular Victorian dish, potted beef will keep for up to a week in the refrigerator when made from very fresh meat and sealed with clarified butter. Chuck and skirt steak are both ideal cuts to use.

butter for greasing
450 g/1 lb lean braising steak, trimmed and cubed
blade of mace
pinch of ground ginger
30 ml/2 tbsp beef stock
75 g/3 oz butter
salt and pepper
melted clarified butter (see Mrs Beeton's Tip, page 25)

Set the oven at 150°C/300°F/gas 2. Combine the beef cubes, mace, ginger and stock in a casserole or oven-proof dish. Cover tightly with buttered greaseproof paper and foil.

Bake for 3½–4 hours, until the meat is very tender. Remove the mace. Mince the meat twice, then pound it well with the butter and any meat juices remaining in the casserole to make a smooth paste. Stir in salt and pepper to taste.

Turn into small pots and cover with clarified butter. When cool, refrigerate the potted beef until the butter is firm.

MAKES ABOUT 450 G/1 LB

MRS BEETON'S TIP

To weight a pâté or terrine cover the top with greaseproof paper and foil, place the dish in an outer container to catch any juices, and add a heavy weight such as cans of food or a well wrapped clean house brick.

PATE MAISON

Home-made pâté is a treat, especially as a gift for some-one who does not have a food processor. Make the pâté the day before presenting it, and add a note indicating that it can be frozen for up to 1 month or refrigerated and consumed within 2–3 days. For a special present, buy an attractive terrine in which to make the pâté.

8–10 rindless back bacon rashers
100 g/4 oz pig's liver, trimmed and coarsely chopped
100 g/4 oz rindless boned belly of pork, coarsely chopped
225 g/8 oz sausagemeat
225 g/8 oz cold cooked rabbit, finely chopped
1 onion, finely chopped
25 g/1 oz fresh white breadcrumbs
1 egg, beaten
15 ml/1 tbsp milk
75 ml/3 fl oz brandy
salt and pepper
3 bay leaves, to garnish

Set the oven at 180°C/350°F/gas 4. Arrange the bay leaves on the base of a 1.25 litre/2¼ pint rectangular ovenproof dish or terrine. Lay the bacon rashers flat on a board, one at a time, and stretch them with the back of a knife until quite thin. Set aside two or three rashers for the topping and use the rest to line the dish, over-lapping them neatly.

Combine the chopped liver, pork, sausagemeat, rab-bit, onion and breadcrumbs in a mixing bowl. Stir in the egg, milk and brandy, with salt and pepper to taste. Spoon the mixture into the lined dish, cover with the reserved bacon rashers and then with a lid or foil. Stand the dish in a roasting tin and add enough hot water to come to within 2.5 cm/1 inch of the rim of the tin.

When cooked, weight the pâté and leave to cool. Chill for 18–24 hours.

MAKES ABOUT 1 KG/2¼ LB

An excellent choice of Christmas gifts: Orange Brandy (page 108), Shortbread (page 54) and Anchovy Relish (page 29).

TERRINE OF DUCK

450 g/1 lb boneless duck meat, minced
125 ml/4 fl oz brandy
450 g/1 lb thinly sliced pork back fat or rindless
streaky bacon rashers
225 g/8 oz rindless boned belly of pork
275 g/10 oz boneless chicken breast
2 shallots, chopped
rind of 1 orange, cut into fine shreds
2.5 ml/½ tsp dried thyme
salt and pepper
3 eggs, beaten

Put the duck meat into a large bowl with the brandy. Cover and marinate for 4–6 hours.

Set the oven at 180°C/350°F/gas 4. Line a 1.4 litre/ 2½ pint ovenproof serving dish with slices of pork fat or bacon, reserving enough to cover the top of the dish.

Mince the belly of pork and chicken together, then add to the duck meat in the bowl. Stir in the shallots, orange rind and herbs, with salt and pepper to taste. Stir in the eggs and mix well. Spoon into the lined dish, smooth and level the surface and cover with the reserved fat or bacon.

Cover the dish with foil and stand the terrine in a roasting tin. Pour boiling water into the outer tin to come almost up to the rim of the dish. Bake for 1¼ hours, or until the terrine shrinks slightly from the sides of the dish and any melted fat on the top is clear. Remove the foil and top layer of fat 15 minutes before the end of cooking time to let the pâté brown slightly.

When cooked, weight the terrine. Cool, then chill for 12 hours.

MAKES ABOUT 1.4 KG/3 LB

MRS BEETON'S TIP

After roasting the pork for the Pork Cheese, pour off excess fat, then use the cooking juices to make gravy. Allow 40 g/1½ oz plain flour to 600 ml/1 pint chicken or vegetable stock. Stir the flour into the residue in the roasting tin and cook, stirring, for 3 minutes. Gradually stir in the stock, bring to the boil, then simmer for 5 minutes, stirring occasionally.

PORK CHEESE

Prepared in one large baking dish or in small pots or ramekins, this pâté-style recipe for cooked pork makes an excellent and unusual gift and if you bake it in a souffle dish, the container will provide a lasting reminder of the occasion.

1.4 kg/3 lb belly of pork, boned
salt and pepper
30 ml/2 tbsp chopped parsley
5 ml/1 tsp chopped fresh thyme or 2.5 ml/½ tsp dried
thyme
2.5 ml/½ tsp chopped rosemary
15 ml/1 tbsp chopped fresh sage or 5 ml/1 tsp dried
sage
2.5 ml/½ tsp ground mace
a little grated nutmeg
grated rind of ½ lemon
300 ml/½ pint pork gravy (see Mrs Beeton's Tip)
butter for greasing

Set the oven at 180°C/350°F/gas 4. Place the pork in a roasting tin and cook for 1½ hours, until cooked through. Leave to cool for about 30 minutes, or until the meat is just cool enough to handle.

Set the oven at 180°C/350°F/gas 4 again. Use a sharp paring knife or fine-bladed knife to cut all the rind off the pork. Chop the meat and fat, either by hand or in a food processor. Do not overprocess the mixture as the pieces should resemble very fine dice. Place the pork in a large bowl. Add plenty of salt and pepper, all the herbs, the mace, nutmeg and lemon rind. If you have a large pestle, use it to pound the meat with the flavouring ingredients; if not, use the back of a sturdy mixing spoon. The more you pound the mixture, the better the texture will be.

When all the ingredients are thoroughly mixed, work in the gravy to bind them together loosely. Good thick gravy is best as it will not make the mixture too runny, more can be incorporated and the cheese will have a good flavour.

Grease a 1.1 litre/2 pint ovenproof dish, for example a soufflé dish or terrine. Turn the mixture into the dish, smooth the surface and cover with foil. Bake for 1¼ hours, then leave to cool completely. Chill overnight.

SERVES 10 TO 12

Savouries and Condiments

Pretty little baskets packed with relishes and sauces make popular gifts, especially when the condiments are all home-made. Presentation is important and an attractive little pot or a neatly labelled jar, complete with fine ribbon and a 'how to serve' tag will look particularly appetising.

ANCHOVY RELISH

Illustrated on page 26

Pack this spicy relish in a small earthenware pot and tie a thin gold ribbon around it, attaching a label with the name of the relish and the suggestion that it be served on fingers of hot toast.

1 (50 g/2 oz) can anchovies
2.5 ml/½ tsp allspice
1.25 ml/¼ tsp grated nutmeg
1.25 ml/¼ tsp ground mace
1.25 ml/¼ tsp ground ginger
pinch of ground cloves
2.5 ml/½ tsp Worcestershire sauce
50 g/2 oz butter, softened
freshly ground black pepper

Pound the anchovies to a paste with the oil from the can. Alternatively, process them in a food processor until smooth. Add the spices individually, pounding in each addition, then mix in the Worcestershire sauce.

Add the butter and work it with the spiced anchovies until thoroughly combined. Add pepper to taste. Transfer to a small pot, cover and chill until ready to use. The paste keeps for up to 4 days in the refrigerator.

MAKES ABOUT 75 G/3 OZ

WELSH RAREBIT

For the many people who think Welsh rarebit is no more exciting than plain cheese on toast, a pot of this savoury mixture will come as a welcome surprise. For a powerful rarebit, replace 15 ml/1 tbsp of the milk or ale mixture with an equivalent amount of whisky. Make a note of the last paragraph of the method on a postcard and attach it to the pot instead of a label.

25 g/1 oz butter
15 ml/1 tbsp plain flour
75 ml/5 tbsp milk or 30 ml/2 tbsp milk and 45 ml/
3 tbsp ale or beer
5 ml/1 tsp French mustard
few drops of Worcestershire sauce
175 g/6 oz Cheddar cheese, grated
salt and pepper

Melt the butter in a saucepan, stir in the flour and cook over gentle heat for 2–3 minutes, stirring constantly. Do not let the flour colour. Stir in the milk and blend to a smooth, thick mixture, then stir in the ale or beer, if used. Add the mustard and Worcestershire sauce.

Gradually add the cheese, stirring after each addition. Remove from the heat as soon as the mixture is smooth. Add salt and pepper to taste. Place in a container, cover and chill when cool.

To use the rarebit, spread the mixture on buttered toast. Place under a preheated hot grill for 2–3 minutes until bubbling and lightly browned. Serve at once.

MAKES ABOUT 225 G/8 OZ

PESTO GENOVESE

2 garlic cloves, roughly chopped
25–40 g/1–1½ oz fresh basil leaves, roughly chopped
25 g/1 oz pine nuts, chopped
40 g/1½ oz Parmesan cheese, grated
juice of 1 lemon
salt and pepper
75–100 ml/3–3½ fl oz olive oil

Combine the garlic, basil leaves, nuts, Parmesan, lemon juice, salt and pepper in a mortar. Pound with a pestle until smooth. Alternatively, process in a blender or food processor. While blending, trickle in the oil as when making mayonnaise, until the sauce is very thick.

SERVES 4

A GOOD SAUCE FOR STEAKS

This sauce may be served neat, as a spicy condiment for grilled steak, or it may be added to gravies and sauces. It is also an excellent ingredient for marinades, and an ideal home-made gift to give with a small item of barbecue equipment, such as tongs or a novelty apron.

25 g/1 oz black peppercorns
15 g/½ oz whole allspice
25 g/1 oz coarse salt
15 g/½ oz grated horseradish
15 g/½ oz pickled onion, chopped
600 ml/1 pint mushroom ketchup

The easiest method of preparing the peppercorns, allspice and salt is to grind them through an empty pepper mill or in an electric spice mill. If this is not a practical option, then pound the spices in a pestle with a mortar. Mix all the ingredients in a screw-topped jar and allow to stand for 2 weeks. Shake the jar occasionally.

Strain the sauce through a muslin-lined sieve and pour it into clean bottles. Cover and label.

MAKES 600 ML/1 PINT

BENTON SAUCE

Fresh horseradish is very useful. Not only is it the basis of an excellent sauce to serve with roast beef, but it also adds piquancy to seafood cocktail sauces and dips. In Mrs Beeton's day, a little horseradish was also added to apple sauce, which was served with pork or beef. This powerful condiment will delight anyone who has a taste for unusual savoury relishes.

30 ml/2 tbsp freshly grated horseradish
10 ml/2 tsp prepared mustard
10 ml/2 tsp caster sugar
125 ml/4 fl oz malt vinegar

Pound the horseradish with the mustard and sugar in a small bowl. Gradually add the vinegar, mixing well.

MAKES ABOUT 150 ML/¼ PINT

HORSERADISH SAUCE

Add the cream only if you know that your gift will be used up quickly. Without the cream, the sauce may be stored in an airtight jar in the refrigerator for at least a couple of weeks.

60 ml/4 tbsp grated horseradish
5 ml/1 tsp caster sugar
5 ml/1 tsp salt
2.5 ml/½ tsp pepper
10 ml/2 tsp prepared mustard
malt vinegar (see method)
45–60 ml/3–4 tbsp single cream (optional)

Mix the horseradish, sugar, salt, pepper and mustard in a non-metallic bowl. Stir in enough vinegar to make a sauce with the consistency of cream. The flavour and appearance will be improved if the quantity of vinegar is reduced, and the single cream added.

MAKES ABOUT 150 ML/¼ PINT

CHRISTOPHER NORTH'S SAUCE

This potent sauce is served as a relish with roast beef, veal or game, or used to pep up gravies. It will keep for weeks in a clean, airtight jar in the refrigerator.

175 ml/6 fl oz port
30 ml/2 tbsp Worcestershire sauce
10 ml/2 tsp mushroom ketchup
10 ml/2 tsp caster sugar
15 ml/1 tbsp lemon juice
1.25 ml/¼ tsp cayenne pepper
2.5 ml/½ tsp salt

Mix all the ingredients together in the top of a double saucepan or a heatproof bowl set over simmering water. Heat gently, without boiling. Serve at once or cool quickly and refrigerate in a closed jar until required.

MAKES ABOUT 250 ML/8 FL OZ

EPICUREAN SAUCE

When writing the label for this sauce, include Mrs Beeton's advice that it be used for steaks, chops and fish.

1 (250 g/9 oz) jar pickled walnuts, mashed with their liquid
150 ml/¼ pint mushroom ketchup
30 ml/2 tbsp soy sauce
30 ml/2 tbsp port
15 ml/1 tbsp white pepper
2 shallots, finely chopped
15 ml/1 tbsp cayenne pepper
15 ml/1 tbsp ground cloves
300 ml/½ pint malt vinegar

Combine all the ingredients in a large, perfectly clean bottle. Seal it tightly. Shake several times daily for about 14 days, then strain the sauce into small bottles, leaving a headspace in each. Seal tightly, label and store in a cool, dry place.

MAKES ABOUT 600 ML/1 PINT

HOT READING SAUCE
Illustrated on page 23

This is a variation on Mrs Beeton's original recipe, which used the liquid from pickled walnuts and a greater proportion of cayenne pepper. The method was more complicated and the sauce was strained after a week's marinating; in the instructions below, the ingredients are cooked together and straining is optional. The sauce is ideal for pepping up stews and meaty sauces or it can be used as a seasoning for salad dressings and dips.

1 (250 g/9 oz) jar pickled walnuts, mashed with their liquid
25 g/1 oz onion, finely chopped
600 ml/1 pint still mineral water
200 ml/7 fl oz soy sauce
15 g/½ oz mustard seeds
15 ml/1 tablespoon anchovy essence
2.5 ml/½ teaspoon cayenne pepper
25 g/1 oz fresh root ginger
2 fresh green chillies
10 bay leaves

Place the mashed walnuts, onion, water, soy sauce, mustard seeds, anchovy essence and cayenne pepper in a saucepan. Peel and finely chop the ginger and add it to the pan. Cut the stalk ends off the chillies, split them and remove their seeds and cores, then chop them finely and add them to the pan. Bring the mixture to the boil, stirring. Reduce the heat, cover the pan and simmer the sauce gently for 1½ hours.

Crush the bay leaves well so that they readily give up their flavour and stir them into the sauce. Pour it into an airtight container and leave to stand for a week. Strain the sauce through muslin if you wish, squeezing all the liquid out of the residue. Pour into bottles, cover with airtight lids and label.

MAKES ABOUT 1.1 LITRES/2 PINTS

QUIN'S SAUCE

You may like to include Mrs Beeton's comment that this is an 'excellent fish sauce' on the label for a jar of this sauce, along with suggestions for using it. It's powerful flavour makes it a versatile condiment for flavouring meat casseroles or rich gravies; it is also an excellent dipping sauce for grilled or barbecued prawns.

6 shallots or 1 small onion, finely chopped
4 pickled walnuts, roughly chopped
30 ml/2 tbsp wine vinegar
150 ml/$\frac{1}{4}$ pint port
300 ml/$\frac{1}{2}$ pint mushroom ketchup
60 ml/4 tbsp anchovy essence
50 ml/2 fl oz soy sauce
1.25 ml/$\frac{1}{4}$ tsp cayenne pepper

Place all the ingredients in a saucepan and bring to the boil, stirring. Reduce the heat and simmer the sauce gently for 15 minutes. Cool slightly, then purée the sauce in a blender or food processor. Pour the sauce into a clean bottle or jar and cover with an airtight lid when completely cold.

MAKES ABOUT 600 ML/1 PINT

Flavoured Vinegars

Vinegar can be spiced and seasoned or flavoured with fruit or herbs to make a variety of versatile condiments. Malt, wine and cider vinegars can all be flavoured and presented in attractive bottles to make interesting culinary gifts. Simply place some fresh herb sprigs, such as rosemary, bay, thyme or mint, in white wine vinegar and leave it to stand for 2–3 weeks for the herbs to impart their flavour to the vinegar. Peeled whole garlic cloves, whole spices, such as cinnamon, cloves or dried red chillies, and finely pared orange or lemon rind may be added to vinegar. These ingredients look attractive and the vinegar may be used in salad dressings or sauces. If you want to spend a little more on the gift, then buy a decorative or coloured-glass bottle. Fresh herb sprigs may be tied around the neck of the bottle, if you wish, as a decorative touch.

SPICED VINEGAR

7 g/$\frac{1}{4}$ oz each of the following spices: cloves, allspice berries, cinnamon sticks (broken into short lengths), fresh root ginger, bruised
1 litre/1$\frac{3}{4}$ pints white or malt vinegar

Fold the spices in a clean cloth. Using a rolling pin, beat lightly to release all the flavour. Combine the spices and vinegar in a large jug, mix well, then pour the liquid into a 1.1 litre/2 pint bottle. Seal the bottle tightly.

Shake the bottle daily for 1 month, then store in a cool dry place for at least 1 month before straining out the spices and returning the vinegar to the clean bottle.

RASPBERRY VINEGAR
Illustrated on page 23

raspberries
white wine vinegar
caster sugar

Clean the fruit thoroughly and measure it by volume. Put it in a bowl and pour in an equal quantity each of vinegar and water. Leave to stand overnight.

Next day, strain the liquid through a fine sieve or jelly bag and measure it again. To each 300 ml/½ pint liquid add 200 ml/7 fl oz caster sugar. Pour the mixture into a saucepan, bring to the boil and boil for 10 minutes. Pour the hot liquid into heated clean bottles and seal at once. Label when cold.

HORSERADISH VINEGAR

600 ml/1 pint white vinegar
50 g/2 oz grated horseradish
15 g/½ oz chopped shallot
2.5 ml/½ tsp salt
pinch of cayenne pepper
25 g/1 oz sugar

Bring the vinegar to the boil in a saucepan. Combine all the remaining ingredients in a heatproof bowl. When the vinegar boils, pour it into the bowl. Cover and set aside to cool.

Bottle the mixture and store for 10 days. It may then be used unstrained as horseradish sauce. To store the vinegar for longer than 10 days, strain it into a clean pan, bring to the boil and pour into heated bottles. Seal securely.

MAKES ABOUT 600 ML/1 PINT

CRANBERRY VINEGAR

2 kg/4½ lb sound ripe cranberries
2.5 litres/4½ pints white wine vinegar
800 g/1¾ lb sugar for every 1 litre/1¾ pints of liquid

Put the fruit in a large, preferably earthenware, bowl. Add the vinegar, cover with a clean cloth and leave to stand in a cool place for 10 days, stirring daily. Strain the liquid through a fine sieve or jelly bag, measure its volume and pour it into a pan.

Stir in the sugar, bring to the boil and boil steadily for 10 minutes or until the mixture is syrupy when a small quantity is tested by cooling on a plate. Skim, bottle and seal at once. Label when cold.

MAKES ABOUT 3.5 LITRES/6 PINTS

STONE FRUIT VINEGAR

Any good quality ripe fruit with stones may be used for this vinegar. Choose from apricots, cherries, damsons, greengages, peaches or plums. Measure by volume as suggested below.

3 litres/5¼ pints fruits with stones
1 litre/1¾ pints white vinegar
800 g/1¾ lb sugar

Halve the fruit, leaving the stones in place, and put it in a large bowl. Add the vinegar, cover with a clean cloth and leave to stand in a cool place for 6 days. Stir the mixture and press down the fruit with a wooden spoon once a day. Finally press the fruit again and strain the liquid through a fine sieve or jelly bag into a saucepan.

Stir in the sugar, bring to the boil and boil steadily for 15 minutes, or until the mixture is syrupy when a small quantity is tested by cooling on a plate. Skim, bottle and seal at once. Label when cold.

MAKES ABOUT 2.8 LITRES/5 PINTS

Salad Dressings

At the height of summer, a basket of freshly picked garden produce makes a welcome gift for those who do not have a vegetable patch. Fresh salad vegetables and herbs, packed with a jar of home-made dressing, look wholesome and inviting. The ingredients in the recipes may be doubled or increased as necessary to make enough dressing to fill the chosen bottle, but keep the proportions of ingredients the same.

FRENCH DRESSING

salt and pepper
pinch of mustard powder
pinch of caster sugar
30 ml/2 tbsp wine vinegar
90 ml/6 tbsp olive oil or a mixture of olive and
sunflower oil

Mix the salt and pepper, mustard and sugar in a small bowl. Add the vinegar and whisk until the sugar has dissolved. Whisk in the oil and check the dressing for salt and pepper. Pour it into a bottle, cover and label.

MAKES ABOUT 125 ML/4 FL OZ

CLARET DRESSING

1 garlic clove, crushed
125 ml/4 fl oz claret
5 ml/1 tsp lemon juice
5 ml/1 tsp finely chopped shallot or onion
salt and pepper

Mix all the ingredients in a screw-topped jar. Close the jar tightly and shake vigorously until well blended; then allow to stand overnight. Shake, strain and pour into an attractive bottle. Cover tightly and label.

MAKES ABOUT 150 ML/¼ PINT

VINAIGRETTE DRESSING

90 ml/6 tablespoons olive oil
salt and pepper
pinch of mustard powder
pinch of caster sugar
30 ml/2 tbsp white wine vinegar
10 ml/2 tsp finely chopped gherkin
5 ml/1 tsp finely chopped onion or chives
5 ml/1 tsp finely chopped parsley
5 ml/1 tsp finely chopped capers
5 ml/1 tsp finely chopped fresh tarragon or chervil

Mix all the ingredients in a screw-topped jar. Close the jar tightly and shake vigorously until well blended; then allow to stand for at least 1 hour. Shake again and pour into an attractive bottle. Cover tightly and label.

MAKES ABOUT 125 ML/4 FL OZ

GREEN REMOULADE

This is a dressing that should be used within 1–2 days of preparation. It is a tempting gift for a single person. Pack in a small serving dish and cover tightly.

3 good sprigs of parsley
2.5 ml/½ tsp sugar
3 hard-boiled egg yolks
2.5 ml/½ tsp made mustard
salt and pepper
15 ml/1 tbsp tarragon vinegar
45 ml/3 tbsps olive oil

Chop the parsley, then sprinkle the sugar over it and continue to chop until it is very fine. Pound it with the egg yolks, mustard, salt and pepper to make a paste. This can be done in a blender, mortar or in a basin, using the back of a mixing spoon. Gradually work in the tarragon vinegar, then slowly work in the olive oil, drop by drop, to make a creamy dressing.

MAKES ABOUT 125 ML/4 FL OZ

LEMON AND BASIL DRESSING

grated rind and juice of 1 lemon
45 ml/3 tbsp cider vinegar
10 ml/2 tsp honey
salt and pepper
5 ml/1 tsp wholegrain mustard
150 ml/¼ pint olive oil
12 large basil leaves

Mix the lemon rind and juice, vinegar, honey, salt and pepper and mustard in a screw-topped jar. Shake well until the ingredients are thoroughly combined. Add the olive oil in three or four batches, shaking well after each addition. Finely shred the basil leaves into the jar, mix lightly, then pour the dressing into a clean jar or bottle and cover with an airtight lid.

MAKES ABOUT 250 ML/8 FL OZ

Savoury Butters

Make savoury butters with unsalted butter for freezing; salted butter for keeping well in the refrigerator. Savoury butters are delicious on grilled fish or meat, with baked jacket potatoes or tossed with pasta. For a special gift, combine a pack of one of the more unusual types of pasta (such as asparagus flavour or dried mushroom pasta) with a pot of savoury butter.

HERB BUTTER

Illustrated on page 23

Herb butter may be prepared using one or more herbs. When mixing herbs, balance strong and mild types. Although dried herbs may be used, fresh ones give a superior flavour. Parsley and dill work well.

100 g/4 oz butter, softened
45 ml/3 tbsp chopped parsley
5 ml/1 tsp chopped fresh thyme
salt and pepper

Beat the butter until creamy in a small bowl. Add the herbs, beating until well combined. Add salt to taste and a small pinch of pepper. Press into small pots, tapping the pots while filling to knock out all the air. Cover and refrigerate until required. Use within 2 days.

MAKES 100 G/4 OZ

HORSERADISH BUTTER

15 ml/1 tbsp grated fresh or bottled horseradish
50 g/2 oz butter, softened • lemon juice

If using bottled horseradish, put it in a colander, rinse it under cold water, then pat dry with absorbent kitchen paper. Beat the butter in a small bowl until light and fluffy. Gradually work in the horseradish. Add lemon juice to taste. Cover and chill until required.

MAKES ABOUT 65 G/2½ OZ

— Baker's Delight —

Breads and Pastries

Home-made pastries are something of a treat
these days and the filo pastries in this chapter are
easily packed to make an excellent savoury gift.
Take advantage of the fine selection of baskets
available in high street shops to prepare an
unusual present, filling one with golden crusty
bread instead of the usual dried flowers or
arrangement of fruit.

FILO AND FETA TRIANGLES

Arrange these pastries in an attractive basket lined
with a napkin or two or three layers of white tissue.
Cover with cling film and label them with a freezing
note, as they will keep well in the freezer for 2–3
months. Add the suggestion that the filo pastries be
served warm.

225 g/8 oz feta cheese
5 ml/1 tsp dried oregano
1 spring onion, chopped
pepper
4 sheets of filo pastry
50 g/2 oz butter, melted

Set the oven at 190°C/375°F/gas 5. Mash the feta with
the oregano in a bowl, then mix in the spring onion
and pepper to taste.

Lay a sheet of filo pastry on a clean, dry surface and
brush it with melted butter. Cut the sheet widthways
into 9 strips. Place a little feta mixture at one end of
the first strip, leaving the corner of the pastry free of
filling. Fold the corner over the feta mixture to cover it
in a triangular shape, then fold the mixture over and
over to wrap it in several layers of pastry, making a
small triangular-shaped pasty.

Repeat with the other strips of pastry. Cut and fill
the remaining sheets in the same way to make 36
triangular pastries. Place these on baking sheets and
brush any remaining butter over them.

Bake for about 10 minutes, until the filo pastry is
crisp and golden. Transfer the triangles to a wire rack
to cool.

MAKES 36

SHAPES AND FILLINGS

The feta filling used in the triangles is a Greek special-
ity. A variety of other fillings may be used and the filo
pastry shaped in other ways.

Instead of cutting strips, the pastry may be cut into
squares (about 6 per sheet). The filling should be
placed in the middle of the squares, and the pastry
folded into neat oblong parcels. Oblong pieces of filo
(about 4 per sheet) may be folded into neat squares.
Alternatively, pastry squares may be gathered up
around the filling to form small bundles. The butter
coating keeps the bundles closed when the filo is
pressed together. For strength, the filo may be used
double. These are more difficult to transport than triangles or parcels, so should be packed with care, on
crumpled tissue or absorbent kitchen paper.

SAVOURY AND SWEET FILLINGS

Spinach and Cheese Thoroughly drained cooked
spinach may be used with or without the cheese.
Flavour plain spinach with chopped spring onion and
grated nutmeg.
Chicken or Ham Chopped cooked chicken or ham
are tasty fillings for filo. Combine them with a little
low-fat soft cheese.
Apricot Apricot halves (drained canned or fresh)
topped with a dot of marmalade make good sweet filo
pastries. Dust them with icing sugar after baking.
Apple and Almond Mix some ground almonds into
cold, sweetened apple purée. Use to fill triangles or
squares.

MINCE PIES
Illustrated on page 76

• •

Mince pies are a favourite pre-Christmas gift. Pack them in a basket or box lined with layers of red, green and white tissue (place the white tissue next to the pies), seal them in a polythene bag and use red and green satin ribbon double to tie a lavish bow around the parcel.

350-450 g/12-16 oz Mincemeat (page 73)
icing or caster sugar for dredging

RICH SHORT CRUST PASTRY
300 g/10 oz plain flour
175 g/6 oz butter
25 g/1 oz caster sugar
1 egg yolk

Set the oven at 200°C/400°F/gas 6. To make the pastry, sift the flour into a bowl. Rub in the butter, then stir in the caster sugar. Using a fork, lightly beat the egg yolk with 30 ml/2 tbsp cold water, then mix this liquid into the rubbed-in ingredients to bind them together into a short dough. Press the dough together to a ball with your fingertips.

Roll out just over half the pastry on a lightly floured surface and cut out circles to line patty tins. Re-roll the pastry trimmings with the remaining unrolled pastry and cut out slightly smaller circles to use as lids.

Place a spoonful of mincemeat in each pastry case. Dampen the edges of the lids and place them on the pies, dampened sides down. Press the edges well to seal them and make a small hole in the top of each pie with the point of a knife. Holly leaves may be stamped out of pastry trimmings, if liked, and brushed with a little water, then placed on top of the pies.

Brush the pies with a little milk and bake for 15-20 minutes, or until golden brown. Leave the pies in the tin for 2-3 minutes, then gently ease them out using a small palette knife and transfer them to a wire rack to cool. Dredge with icing or caster sugar.

MAKES ABOUT 15

BUTTERS TO SERVE WITH MINCE PIES
Either of these butters makes a perfect partner for a gift of home-baked mince pies. Make a note of the suggested storage time (2-3 weeks in the refrigerator) on a gift tag and tie it around the neck of the jar.

BRANDY BUTTER
Illustrated on page 76

• •

50 g/2 oz unsalted butter
100 g/4 oz caster sugar
15-30 ml/1-2 tbsp brandy

In a bowl, cream the butter until soft. Gradually beat in the sugar until the mixture is pale and light. Work in the brandy, a little at a time, taking care not to allow the mixture to curdle. Spoon the butter into a jar, teasing it down into the base with the point of a knife to eliminate any pockets of air, then cover and chill.

MAKES ABOUT 150 G/5 OZ

CUMBERLAND RUM BUTTER

• •

100 g/4 oz unsalted butter
100 g/4 oz soft light brown sugar
30 ml/2 tbsp rum
2.5 ml/½ tsp grated orange rind
grated nutmeg

Put the butter in a bowl and cream it until very soft and light in colour. Crush any lumps in the sugar. Work it into the butter until completely blended in.

Work the rum into the butter, a few drops at a time, take care not to let the mixture separate. Mix in the orange rind. Taste the mixture and add a little grated nutmeg.

Spoon the rum butter into a screw-topped jar and cover tightly. Chill until required.

MAKES ABOUT 225 G/8 OZ

KULICH

This is a traditional Russian Easter bread, baked in deep round moulds.

fat for greasing
450 g/1 lb strong white flour
2.5 ml/½ tsp salt
1.25 ml/¼ tsp powdered saffron
1 sachet fast-action easy-blend dried yeast
50 g/2 oz caster sugar
100 g/4 oz ground almonds
50 g/2 oz chopped mixed peel
25 g/1 oz glacé cherries, chopped
25 g/1 oz candied pineapple or angelica, chopped
50 g/2 oz blanched almonds
250 ml/8 fl oz milk
75 g/3 oz butter
3 egg yolks plus 1 white
flour for kneading

Grease a 20 cm/8 inch round deep cake tin. Wrap a double-thick band of greaseproof paper around the outside of the tin, to stand about 5 cm/2 inches above its rim. Grease the inside of the paper.

Sift the flour and salt into a bowl. Stir in the saffron, yeast, sugar, ground almonds, mixed peel, cherries, pineapple or angelica and blanched almonds. Make a well in the middle of these dry ingredients.

Measure 100 ml/3½ fl oz water into a saucepan. Add the milk and butter to the water and heat gently until the butter has melted. Allow the liquid to stand for a few minutes, if necessary, until it is no more than hand-hot, then pour it into the well in the dry ingredients. Add the egg yolks and stir them with the liquid until well mixed, then gradually work in the dry mixture to make a stiff batter. Whisk the egg white until stiff but not dry, then mix it into the batter: the best way to work the batter is using the palm of your hand. When the egg white is mixed into the batter, beat it with your hand, holding the bowl at a slight angle and cradling it with one hand and forearm, then using your other hand like a paddle. As the dough becomes more elastic and you develop a rhythm for the mixing, the process becomes slightly easier. Continue for about 10 minutes, or until the mixture feels quite elastic.

Turn the mixture into the tin. Place the tin in a large, lightly oiled polythene bag. Leave in a warm place until doubled in bulk – this will take longer than when making ordinary bread as the additional ingredients slow down the process.

Set the oven at 180°C/350°F/gas 4. Bake the loaf for about 40 minutes, until well risen and deep golden brown on top. Leave to cool in the tin for 2 minutes, then transfer to a wire rack to cool completely.

MAKES 1 KULICH

CHALLAH

fat for greasing
800 g/1¾ lb strong white flour
10 ml/2 tsp salt
10 ml/2 tsp sugar
1 sachet fast-action easy-blend dried yeast
100 g/4 oz butter or margarine
2 eggs, beaten
flour for kneading
beaten egg for glazing

Grease two baking sheets. Mix the flour, salt, sugar and yeast in a large bowl. Rub in the butter or margarine, then make a well in the middle of the dry ingredients.

Add 400 ml/14 fl oz hand-hot water and the eggs, then gradually stir in the dry ingredients to make a soft dough. Turn on to a lightly floured surface and knead for about 10 minutes until the dough is smooth and elastic.

Cut the dough into two equal portions. Cut one of these into two equal pieces and roll these into long strands 30–35 cm/12–14 inches in length. Arrange the two strands in a cross on a flat surface. Take the two opposite ends of the bottom strand and cross them over the top strand in the centre. Repeat this, using the other strand. Cross each strand alternately, building up the plait vertically, until all the dough is used up. Gather the short ends together and pinch firmly. Lay the challah on its side and place on the prepared baking sheet. Repeat using the second portion. Cover with lightly oiled polythene and leave in a warm place until doubled in size.

Set the oven at 220°C/425°F/gas 7. Brush the loaves with beaten egg and bake them for 35–40 minutes, until the loaves are golden brown and sound hollow when tapped on the bottom.

MAKES 2 (800 G/1¾ LB) LOAVES

BAGELS

The bagels may be frozen after poaching but before baking, then they should be baked after thawing. Alternatively, they may be fully cooked before cooling and freezing; either way or hot from the oven, a batch of home-made bagels is a most acceptable gift – particularly when accompanied by a pack of smoked salmon, a pot of soured cream and a bottle of champagne for a very special occasion.

fat for greasing
400 g/14 oz strong-white flour
5 ml/1 tsp salt
30 ml/2 tbsp sugar
1 sachet fast-action easy-blend dried yeast
50 g/2 oz margarine
1 egg, separated
flour for kneading
poppy seeds

Grease a baking sheet. Sift the flour into a large bowl. Stir in the salt, sugar and yeast, and make a well in the middle of these dry ingredients. Measure 250 ml/8 fl oz water into a saucepan and add the margarine. Heat gently until the fat has melted. Leave the liquid to stand, if necessary, until it is hand-hot.

Whisk the egg white lightly, then add to the flour with the margarine liquid. Mix to a soft dough, then turn the dough out on to a floured surface and knead it for about 10 minutes, until it is smooth and elastic. Cut off 25 g/1 oz pieces of dough. Roll each piece into a sausage shape 15–20 cm/6–8 inches in length; then form this into a ring, pinching the ends securely together. Place the rings on a well-floured surface, cover loosely with lightly oiled cling film or a polythene bag and leave until they have risen slightly.

Set the oven at 190°C/375°F/gas 5. Heat a large saucepan of water to just under boiling point. Drop in the bagels, a few at a time and poach them on one side for 2 minutes, then turn them over and cook on the other side for about 2 minutes or until they are light and have risen slightly. Place on the prepared baking sheet.

Beat the egg yolk, brush it over the top of the bagels and sprinkle with poppy seeds. Bake for 20–30 minutes, until golden brown and crisp.

MAKES 28

BRIOCHES

fat for greasing
400 g/14 oz strong white flour
5 ml/1 tsp salt
50 g/2 oz butter
1 sachet fast-action easy-blend dried yeast
2 eggs, beaten
flour for kneading
beaten egg for glazing

Grease twelve 7.5 cm/3 inch brioche or deep bun tins. Sift the flour and salt into a large bowl. Rub in the butter, then stir in the yeast. Make a well in the middle of the dry ingredients and add the eggs with 45 ml/3 tbsp hot water. The water should feel very hot to the touch. Stir the water into the eggs, then mix in the flour to form a soft dough. Turn on to a floured surface and knead for about 10 minutes or until the dough is smooth and elastic. Cut the dough into 12 equal pieces. Cut off one-quarter of each piece used. Form the larger piece into a ball and place in a prepared tin. Firmly press a hole in the centre and place the remaining quarter as a knob in the centre. Place the tins on a baking sheet and cover with a large, lightly oiled polythene bag. Leave in a warm place until the dough is well risen, light and puffy.

Set the oven at 230°C/450°F/gas 8. Brush the brioches with beaten egg and bake for 15–20 minutes, until golden brown. Cool on a wire rack.

MAKES 12

HOT CROSS BUNS

Nothing can match a batch of home-baked hot cross buns, made with a good seasoning of spice. They are an excellent Easter offering instead of chocolate eggs for adults and are greatly appreciated by elderly friends who no longer do much baking.

flour for dusting
125 ml/4 fl oz milk
400 g/14 oz strong white flour
5 ml/1 tsp salt
7.5 ml/1½ tsp ground mixed spice
2.5 ml/½ tsp ground cinnamon
2.5 ml/½ tsp grated nutmeg
50 g/2 oz butter
50 g/2 oz caster sugar
1 sachet fast-action easy-blend dried yeast
100 g/4 oz currants
50 g/2 oz chopped mixed peel
1 egg, beaten
flour for kneading

GLAZE
30 ml/2 tbsp milk
40 g/1½ oz caster sugar

Warm the milk with 75 ml/3 fl oz water until it is hand hot. Mix the flour, salt and spices in a bowl. Rub in the butter. Stir in the caster sugar, yeast and dried fruit. Make a well in the dry ingredients, then add the milk mixture and egg; mix to a soft dough. Turn on to a lightly floured surface and knead for about 10 minutes, until smooth and elastic.

Cut the dough into 12 equal pieces and shape each into a round bun. Place on a floured baking sheet. With a sharp knife slash a cross on the top of each bun. Cover with oiled polythene and leave in a warm place until doubled in size.

Set the oven at 220°C/425°F/gas 7. Bake the buns for 15–20 minutes, until golden. To make the glaze, boil the milk, sugar and 30 ml/2 tbsp water together in a small saucepan for 6 minutes. Brush the glaze over the hot buns as soon as they are removed from the oven, then transfer them to a wire rack to cool.

MAKES 12

IRISH SODA BREAD

A neat loaf of soda bread, with a sharp-cut cross on the top, makes an attractive present. It should be presented on the day it is made or it can be frozen as soon as it is cold and given in its frozen state, ready to be placed straight in the freezer.

fat for greasing
575 g/1¼ lb plain flour
5 ml/1 tsp bicarbonate of soda
5 ml/1 tsp salt
5 ml/1 tsp cream of tartar (if using fresh milk)
300 ml/½ pint buttermilk or soured milk or fresh milk
flour for dusting

Grease a large baking sheet. Set the oven at 190–200°C/375–400°F/gas 5–6. Mix all the dry ingredients in a bowl, then make a well in the centre. Add enough milk to make a fairly slack dough, pouring it in almost all at once, not spoonful by spoonful. Mix with a wooden spoon, lightly and quickly.

With floured hands, place the mixture on a lightly floured surface and flatten the dough into a round about 2.5 cm/1 inch thick. Turn on to the prepared baking sheet. Make a large cross in the surface with a floured knife to make it heat through evenly.

Bake for about 40 minutes. To test if the loaf is ready, pierce the centre with a thin skewer; it should come out clean. Wrap the loaf in a clean tea-towel to keep it soft until required. (A smart new tea-towel could be part of the present.)

MAKES 1 (750 G/1¾ LB) LOAF

CHRISTMAS STOLLEN

This is the classic German Christmas bread. Pack it in a tightly closed polythene bag, with a double bow of red and gold ribbon to conceal a wire tie.

fat for greasing
1 kg/2¼ lb plain flour
5 ml/1 tsp salt
2 sachets fast-action easy-blend dried yeast
250 g/9 oz caster sugar
grated rind and juice of 1 lemon
350 g/12 oz butter
200 ml/7 fl oz lukewarm milk
2 egg yolks
500 g/18 oz seedless raisins
225 g/8 oz sultanas
150 g/5 oz blanched slivered almonds
100 g/4 oz chopped mixed peel
flour for dusting
50 g/2 oz unsalted butter
icing sugar for dusting

Grease two baking sheets. Mix the flour, salt and yeast in a bowl. Stir in the sugar and lemon rind, then make a well in the middle of these dry ingredients. Heat the butter and milk together gently until the butter has melted and the mixture is hand-hot; allow the liquid to cool slightly, if necessary, before pouring it into the dry ingredients. Stir in the lemon juice and egg yolks, then gradually work in the flour to make a dough. Turn the dough out on to a floured surface and knead for about 10 minutes, until it is smooth and elastic.

Mix the raisins, sultanas, almonds and mixed peel. Knead the fruit and nut mixture into the dough by flattening the dough and adding a handful of the mixture, then folding the dough over and kneading it again.

When all the fruit mixture is incorporated, divide the dough in half. Roll each half into a pointed oval shape. Lay each on a prepared baking sheet. Working on one piece of dough at a time, centre a rolling pin along its length. Roll half the dough lightly from the centre outwards. Brush the thinner rolled half with a little water and fold the other half over it, leaving a margin of about 5 cm/2 inches all around which allows the dough to rise. Press well together; the water will bind the dough.

Cover the stollen with lightly oiled polythene and leave to rise in a warm place until both have doubled in bulk. Set the oven at 190°C/375°F/gas 5.

Melt the unsalted butter and brush it over both stollen. Bake for about 1 hour, until golden. Dredge the stollen thickly with icing sugar and return them to the oven for 5 minutes. Then transfer them to a wire rack to cool. Keep for a day before cutting.

The stollen will remain fresh for many weeks if well wrapped in greaseproof paper and stored in an airtight container or polythene bag.

MAKES 2 LOAVES, ABOUT 24 SLICES EACH

CHERRY BREAD

fat for greasing
200 g/7 oz strong white flour
2.5 ml/½ tsp salt
5 ml/1 tsp sugar
25 g/1 oz butter or margarine
1 sachet fast-action easy-blend dried yeast
100 ml/3½ fl oz milk
1 egg, beaten
flour for kneading
75 g/3 oz glacé cherries
milk for glazing

Grease a 15 cm/6 inch square cake tin. Mix the flour, salt and sugar in a bowl. Rub in the butter or margarine. Stir in the yeast. Heat the milk until hand hot. Add to the flour mixture with the beaten egg and mix to a soft dough. Turn on to a lightly floured surface and knead for about 10 minutes or until smooth and elastic.

Chop the cherries roughly and knead them into the risen dough until well distributed. Press the dough into the prepared cake tin and place the tin in a large, lightly oiled polythene bag. Leave in a warm place until the dough reaches just above the edge of the tin.

Set the oven at 220°C/425°F/gas 7. Brush the bread with a little milk and bake for 10 minutes, them lower the oven temperature to 190°C/375°F/gas 5. Continue baking for 15 – 25 minutes, until golden brown.

MAKES 1 (400 G/14 OZ) LOAF

SWEET ALMOND BREAD

A layer of almond paste is baked into this bread.

fat for greasing
200 g/7 oz strong white flour
2.5 ml/½ tsp salt
5 ml/1 tsp sugar
25 g/1 oz butter or margarine
1 sachet fast-action easy-blend dried yeast
100 ml/3½ fl oz milk
1 egg, beaten
flour for kneading
milk for glazing
sifted icing sugar for dredging

ALMOND PASTE
75 g/3 oz icing sugar, sifted
75 g/3 oz ground almonds
5 ml/1 tsp lemon juice
few drops of almond essence
beaten egg white

Grease a baking sheet. Mix the flour, salt and sugar in a bowl. Rub in the butter or margarine, then stir in the yeast. Heat the milk until hand hot, then pour it into the flour mixture, add the egg and mix to a soft dough. Turn on to a lightly floured surface and knead for about 10 minutes or until the dough is smooth and elastic.

To make the almond paste, mix the icing sugar, ground almonds, lemon juice and almond essence with enough egg white to bind the mixture together.

Roll out the dough on a lightly floured surface to a 25 cm/10 inch round. Break the almond paste into lumps and sprinkle them on to half the dough round. Fold the uncovered half of the dough over to cover the paste. Press the edges of dough firmly together. Brush the surface with milk. Place on the prepared baking sheet and cover with oiled polythene. Leave in a warm place until doubled in size. Set the oven at 220°C/425°F/gas 7.

Bake for 10 minutes, then lower the oven temperature to 190°C/375°F/gas 5. Continue baking for 15–25 minutes, until the bread is golden brown. When cold, dredge the bread with a little sifted icing sugar.

MAKES 1 (400 G/14 OZ) LOAF

Teabreads

Those who are not over-fond of cake often favour a slice of buttered teabread. When packing these delicious breads, remember to add a label with the suggestion that they be served sliced and buttered.

BANANA AND WALNUT BREAD

Place the teabread on a folded tea-towel and pack both inside a polythene bag, tying the bag with ribbon to match the tea-towel and adding a label.

fat for greasing
3 ripe bananas
50 g/2 oz walnuts, chopped
200 g/7 oz self-raising flour
5 ml/1 tsp baking powder
1.25 ml/¼ tsp bicarbonate of soda
125 g/4½ oz caster sugar
75 g/3 oz soft margarine
grated rind of ½ lemon
2 eggs
50 g/2 oz seedless raisins

Grease a 23 × 13 × 7.5 cm/9 × 5 × 3 inch loaf tin. Set the oven at 180°C/350°F/gas 4. Mash the bananas.

Mix all the ingredients in a large bowl. Beat for about 3 minutes by hand using a wooden spoon, or for 2 minutes in an electric mixer, until smooth. Put the mixture into the prepared loaf tin. Bake for 1 hour 10 minutes, or until firm to the touch. Cool on a wire rack.

MAKES ABOUT 12 SLICES

MALT BREAD

fat for greasing
400 g/14 oz self-raising flour
10 ml/2 tsp bicarbonate of soda
100 g/4 oz sultanas or seedless raisins
250 ml/8 fl oz milk
60 ml/4 tbsp golden syrup
60 ml/4 tbsp malt extract
2 eggs

Grease a 23 × 13 × 7.5 cm/9 × 5 × 3 inch loaf tin. Set the oven at 190°C/375°F/gas 5. Sift the flour and bicarbonate of soda into a large bowl. Add the dried fruit. Warm the milk, syrup and malt extract in a saucepan. Beat in the eggs. Stir the mixture into the flour. Put into the prepared loaf tin.

Bake for 40–50 minutes, until a skewer pushed into the bread comes out clean. Cool on a wire rack.

MAKES 12 SLICES

DATE AND CHEESE BREAD

fat for greasing
flour for dusting
200 g/7 oz stoned dates
1 egg
100 g/4 oz mild cheese, grated
175 g/6 oz plain flour
5 ml/1 tsp bicarbonate of soda
1.25 ml/¼ tsp salt
50 g/2 oz granulated sugar
50 g/2 oz soft light brown sugar

Grease and flour a 23 × 13 × 7.5 cm/9 × 5 × 3 inch loaf tin. Set the oven at 160°C/325°F/gas 3. Place the dates in a bowl and pour 125 ml/4 fl oz boiling water on to them. Allow to stand for 5 minutes.

Mix in the egg, then add the cheese. Sift the flour, bicarbonate of soda and salt into the date mixture. Add both sugars and mix thoroughly. Put the mixture into the prepared loaf tin.

Bake for about 50 minutes, until a skewer pushed into the centre comes out clean. Cool.

MAKES ABOUT 12 SLICES

NORTH RIDING BREAD

This rich, dark fruit bread tastes even better if kept in a tin for a week before being served.

fat for greasing
400 g/14 oz plain flour
2.5 ml/½ tsp salt
15 ml/1 tbsp baking powder
2.5 ml/½ tsp grated nutmeg
100 g/4 oz lard
150 g/5 oz demerara sugar
150 g/5 oz currants
150 g/5 oz seedless raisins
75 g/3 oz chopped mixed peel
15 ml/1 tbsp black treacle
2.5 ml/½ tsp almond essence
250 ml/8 fl oz milk

Grease a 23 × 13 × 7.5 cm/9 × 5 × 3 inch loaf tin. Set the oven at 190°C/375°F/gas 5.

Sift the flour, salt, baking powder and nutmeg into a large bowl. Rub in the lard. Add the sugar and dried fruit. Stir the treacle and almond essence into the milk and mix into the dry ingredients to give a soft dough. Put the mixture into the prepared loaf tin.

Bake for 45–50 minutes, until a skewer pushed into the bread comes out clean. Cool on a wire rack, then store in a tin.

MAKES ABOUT 12 SLICES

FREEZER TIP

Freeze teabreads and loaf cakes cut into slices. Separate the slices with freezer film, then re-shape the loaf and pack it in a polythene bag. Individual slices may be removed as required, making this an ideal gift for someone who lives alone. Either give the teabread in its frozen state and make sure it is put straight into the freezer, or pack it ready for freezing.

Cakes Galore

No special celebration is complete without a cake, and even when there is no occasion to commemorate, a home-baked cake is a welcome surprise. Instructions for icing and decorations are given in a few instances, but for the most part the recipes in this chapter concentrate on the cake itself.

MINIATURE FRUIT CAKES
Illustrated opposite
....

One of these small cakes would make an ideal gift for someone living alone. Once the basic cake has been covered with almond paste and sugar paste, add bought decorations appropriate to the occasion, or follow the specific suggestions below.

....

400 g/14 oz currants
200 g/7 oz raisins
200 g/7 oz sultanas
200 g/7 oz butter, softened
200 g/7 oz moist dark brown sugar
grated rind of 1 lemon
40 g/1½ oz almonds, shelled
40 g/1½ oz citrus peel, chopped
75 g/3 oz glacé cherries
200 g/7 oz plain flour
2.5 ml/½ tsp ground mixed spice
3 eggs, beaten
15 ml/1 tbsp black treacle

DECORATION
675 g/1½ lb almond paste
675 g/1½ lb sugar paste

....

Use two 10 cm/4 inch round cake tins as containers for baking the cakes. Alternatively, wash and dry two empty 822 g/1 lb 3 oz cans, for example fruit cans. Set the oven at 150°C/300°F/gas 2. Line and grease the tins or cans.

Mix the currants, raisins and sultanas. Cream the butter, sugar and lemon rind until very soft. Beat in the almonds and the citrus peel. Wash and dry the cherries, then roughly chop them and toss them with a little of the measured flour. Sift the remaining flour with the spice and toss a little with the mixed dried fruit. Beat the eggs and treacle into the creamed mixture, adding a spoonful of the flour occasionally to prevent the mixture from curdling. Fold in the remaining flour. Lastly fold in the dried fruit and the cherries.

Turn the mixture into the tins or cans and smooth the top of each with the back of a wetted metal spoon, hollowing out the centre slightly. Cook for 1½ hours. Insert a clean metal skewer into the centre of each cake to test if it is cooked: if it comes out free of mixture, the cake is ready. If there is any sticky mixture on the skewer bake the cakes for a little longer.

Leave the cakes to cool in the tins or cans for at least an hour, then transfer them to a wire rack to cool completely. Do not remove the lining paper. Wrap the cakes, still in the lining paper, in fresh greaseproof paper and store them in an airtight tin.

Cover the cakes with almond paste and sugar paste. Roll out 2 thin ropes of sugar paste and place one around the base of each cake, joining it at the back to make a neat edge.

The iced cakes can be decorated very simply, with bought sugar flowers, crystallized violets or bought decorations. Silk flowers or even clean, dry fresh flowers can also be used for decoration. The sugar paste may be patterned using cake modelling tools and crimpers. A simple design can be made by rolling out coloured sugar paste and cutting out shapes such as numerals or figures to indicate the age or name of the recipient. A car can be cut out and painted with food colouring for someone who has successfully passed a driving test; a house can be made for a new home-owner; a Father Christmas or snowman can be made for a Christmas cake (for instructions on how to make a snowman template, see the recipe for Snowmen on page 57).

ABOUT 10–12 PORTIONS EACH
....

Miniature Fruit Cakes are ideal for any occasion, from christenings and birthdays to anniversaries and Christmas.

DUNDEE CAKE

....

fat for greasing
200 g/7 oz plain flour
2.5 ml/½ tsp baking powder
1.25 ml/¼ tsp salt
150 g/5 oz butter
150 g/5 oz caster sugar
4 eggs, beaten
100 g/4 oz glacé cherries, quartered
150 g/5 oz currants
150 g/5 oz sultanas
100 g/4 oz seedless raisins
50 g/2 oz cut mixed peel
50 g/2 oz ground almonds
grated rind of 1 lemon
50 g/2 oz blanched split almonds

....

Home-baked Dundee Cake is a traditional Christmas treat which makes an equally acceptable gift throughout the seasons.

Line and grease an 18 cm/7 inch round cake tin. Set the oven at 180°C/350°F/gas 4. Sift the flour, baking powder and salt into a bowl. In a mixing bowl, cream the butter and sugar together well, and beat in the eggs. Fold the flour mixture, cherries, dried fruit, peel and ground almonds into the creamed mixture. Add the lemon rind and mix well.

Spoon into the prepared tin and make a slight hollow in the centre. Bake for 20 minutes, by which time the hollow should have filled in. Arrange the split almonds on top.

Return the cake to the oven, bake for a further 40–50 minutes, then reduce the temperature to 160°C/325°F/gas 3 and bake for 1 hour more. Cool on a wire rack.

MAKES 1 (18 CM/7 INCH) CAKE

....

BLACK BUN

A very rich, spicy cake with a distinctly peppery tang, this classic mixture is encased in pastry. A black bun would traditionally be served on Twelfth Night or at Hogmanay to celebrate the new year. The cake is best kept in an airtight tin for 1 month before cutting, so this is a useful gift to make for the festive season.

400 g/14 oz plain flour
100 g/4 oz blanched whole almonds, roughly chopped
675 g/1½ lb muscatel raisins, seeded
675 g/1½ lb currants
100 g/4 oz cut mixed peel
200 g/7 oz caster sugar
30 ml/2 tbsp ground ginger
30 ml/2 tbsp ground cinnamon
30 ml/2 tbsp mixed spice
2.5 ml/½ tsp freshly ground black pepper
10 ml/2 tsp bicarbonate of soda
5 ml/1 tsp cream of tartar
350 ml/12 fl oz milk
15 ml/1 tbsp brandy

PASTRY
450 g/1 lb plain flour
225 g/8 oz butter
5 ml/1 tsp baking powder
flour for rolling out
beaten egg for glazing

Sift the flour into a large bowl. Add the almonds, dried fruit, peel, sugar and spices and mix well. Stir in the bicarbonate of soda and the cream of tartar, then moisten with the milk and brandy. Set the oven at 200°C/400°F/gas 6.

Make the pastry. Put the flour into a mixing bowl. Rub in the butter until the mixture resembles fine breadcrumbs, then add the baking powder. Stir in enough water (about 125 ml/4 fl oz) to form a stiff dough. Leave the dough to rest for a few minutes, then roll out on a lightly floured surface to a thickness of about 5 mm/¼ inch. Using three-quarters of the pastry, line a 23 cm/9 inch round cake tin (about 10 cm/4 inches deep), leaving a border around the edges for overlap. Roll out the remaining pastry for the lid.

Fill the pastry-lined tin with the cake mixture, and turn the edges of the pastry over it. Moisten the edges with water, put on the lid and seal. Decorate the pastry with any trimmings, prick with a fork all over the top and brush with the egg.

Bake for 1 hour, then lower the oven temperature to 160°C/325°F/gas 3, cover the top of the bun loosely with paper or foil and continue baking for 2 hours more.

Leave the bun to cool in the tin for 20 minutes, then remove it from the tin and cool completely. Keep for 1 month in an airtight tin before using.

MAKES 1 (23 CM/9 INCH) CAKE

FESTIVAL FRUIT CAKE

fat for greasing
225 g/8 oz plain flour
1.25 ml/¼ tsp salt
2.5 ml/½ tsp baking powder
50 g/2 oz currants
50 g/2 oz sultanas
50 g/2 oz glacé cherries, washed, dried and chopped
50 g/2 oz cut mixed peel
150 g/5 oz butter or margarine
150 g/5 oz caster sugar
2 eggs. beaten
15 ml/1 tbsp milk (optional)

Line and grease an 18 cm/7 inch cake tin. Set the oven at 180°C/350°F/gas 4. Sift the flour, salt and baking powder into a bowl. Stir in the dried fruit, cherries and mixed peel and mix well. Set aside.

Place the butter or margarine in a mixing bowl and beat until very soft. Add the sugar and cream together until light and fluffy. Add the beaten eggs gradually, beating well after each addition. If the mixture shows signs of curdling, add a little of the flour mixture.

Fold in the dry ingredients and fruit lightly but thoroughly, adding the milk if too stiff.

Spoon into the prepared tin, smooth the surface and make a slight hollow in the centre. Bake for 30 minutes, then reduce the oven temperature to 160°C/325°F/gas 3 and bake for 40 minutes more until firm to the touch. Cool on a wire rack.

MAKES 1 (18 CM/7 INCH) CAKE

TWELFTH NIGHT CAKE

The tradition of the Twelfth Night Cake goes back to the days of the early Christian Church and beyond. In the Middle Ages, whoever found the bean in his cake became the 'Lord of Misrule' or 'King' for the festivities of Twelfth Night, with the finder of the pea as his 'Queen'. Finding the bean was thought to bring luck. The tradition survived until near the end of the nineteenth century.

fat for greasing
150 g/5 oz margarine
75 g/3 oz soft dark brown sugar
3 eggs
300 g/11 oz plain flour
60 ml/4 tbsp milk
5 ml/1 tsp bicarbonate of soda
30 ml/2 tbsp golden syrup
2.5 ml/½ tsp mixed spice
2.5 ml/½ tsp ground cinnamon
pinch of salt
50 g/2 oz currants
100 g/4 oz sultanas
100 g/4 oz cut mixed peel
1 dried bean (see above)
1 large dried whole pea (see above)

Line and grease a 15 cm/6 inch round cake tin. Set the oven at 180°C/350°F/gas 4.

In a mixing bowl, cream the margarine and sugar until light and fluffy. Beat in the eggs, one at a time, adding a little flour with each. Warm the milk, add the bicarbonate of soda and stir until dissolved. Add the syrup.

Mix the spices and salt with the remaining flour in a bowl. Add this to the creamed mixture alternately with the flavoured milk. Lightly stir in the dried fruit and peel. Spoon half the cake mixture into the prepared tin, lay the bean and pea in the centre, then cover with the rest of the cake mixture. Bake for about 2 hours. Cool on a wire rack.

MAKES 1 (15 CM/6 INCH) CAKE

SIMNEL CAKE

fat for greasing
200 g/7 oz plain flour
2.5 ml/½ tsp baking powder
1.25 ml/¼ tsp salt
150 g/5 oz butter
150 g/5 oz caster sugar
4 eggs
100 g/4 oz glacé cherries, halved
150 g/5 oz currants
150 g/5 oz sultanas
100 g/4 oz seedless raisins • 50 g/2 oz cut mixed peel
50 g/2 oz ground almonds
grated rind of 1 lemon

FILLING AND DECORATION
450 g/1 lb marzipan or almond paste
30 ml/2 tbsp smooth apricot jam (see method)
1 egg, beaten

Line and grease a 18 cm/7 inch cake tin. Set the oven at 180°C/350°F/gas 4. Sift the flour, baking powder and salt into a bowl. In a mixing bowl, cream the butter and sugar together well and beat in the eggs, adding a little of the flour mixture if necessary. Fold the flour mixture, cherries, dried fruit, peel and ground almonds into the creamed mixture. Add the lemon rind and mix well.

Spoon half the mixture into the prepared tin. Cut one third of the marzipan or almond paste and roll it to a pancake about 1 cm/½ inch thick and slightly smaller than the circumference of the tin. Place it gently on top of the mixture and spoon the remaining cake mixture on top.

Bake for 1 hour, then reduce the oven temperature to 160°C/325°F/gas 3 and bake for 1½ hours more. Cool in the tin, then turn out on a wire rack.

Warm, then sieve the apricot jam. When the cake is cold, divide the remaining almond paste in half. Roll one half to a round with a slightly smaller diameter than the top of the cake. Brush the top of the cake with apricot jam and press the almond paste lightly on to it. Trim the edge neatly.

Make 11 small balls with the remaining paste and place them around the edge of the cake. Brush the balls with the beaten egg and brown under the grill.

MAKES 1 (18 CM/7 INCH) CAKE

BATTENBURG CAKE

This cake is a treat for those who love almond paste and is a good alternative to a simnel cake for an Easter gift.

fat for greasing
100 g/4 oz self-raising flour • pinch of salt
100 g/4 oz butter or margarine
100 g/4 oz caster sugar • 2 eggs
pink food colouring
apricot jam, warmed and sieved
225 g/8 oz marzipan or almond paste

Line and grease a 23 × 18 cm/9 × 7 inch Battenburg tin or use a 23 × 18 cm/9 × 7 inch square cake tin and cut a band of double greaseproof paper to separate the mixture into 2 equal parts. Set the oven at 190°C/375°F/gas 5. Mix the flour and salt in a bowl.

In a mixing bowl, cream the butter or margarine and sugar together until light and fluffy. Add the eggs, one at a time, with a little flour. Stir in, then beat well. Stir in the remaining flour lightly but thoroughly.

Place half the mixture in one half of the tin. Tint the remaining mixture pink, and place it in the other half of the tin. Smooth both mixtures away from the centre towards the outside of the tin.

Bake for 25–30 minutes. Leave the cakes in the tin for a few minutes, then transfer them to a wire rack and peel off the paper. Leave to cool completely.

To finish the Battenburg, cut each slab of cake lengthways into 3 strips. Trim off any crisp edges and rounded surfaces so that all 6 strips are neat and of the same size. Arrange 3 strips with 1 pink strip in the middle. Where the cakes touch, brush with the glaze and press together lightly. Make up the other layer in the same way, using 2 pink with 1 plain strip in the middle. Brush glaze over the top of the base layer and place the second layer on top.

Roll out the marzipan or almond paste thinly into a rectangle the same length as the strips and wide enough to wrap around them. Brush it with glaze and place the cake in the centre. Wrap the paste around the cake and press the edges together lightly. Turn so that the join is underneath; trim the ends. Mark the top of the paste with the back of a knife to make a criss-cross pattern.

MAKES 1 (23 × 18 CM/9 × 7 INCH) CAKE

GINGERBREAD WITH PINEAPPLE

Make this gingerbread at least a week before eating and store in an airtight tin. It is an excellent surprise present for a November 5th party.

fat for greasing
200 g/7 oz plain flour
1.25 ml/¼ tsp salt
15 ml/1 tbsp ground ginger
2.5 ml/½ tsp bicarbonate of soda
50 g/2 oz crystallized ginger, chopped
50 g/2 oz crystallized pineapple, chopped
75 g/3 oz butter or margarine
50 g/2 oz soft light brown sugar
50 g/2 oz golden syrup
50 g/2 oz black treacle
1 egg
milk (see method)

Line and grease a 15 cm/6 inch square tin. Set the oven at 160°C/325°F/gas 3.

Sift the flour, salt, ground ginger and bicarbonate of soda into a mixing bowl. Stir in the crystallized fruit. Warm the butter or margarine with the sugar, syrup and treacle in a saucepan until the fat has melted. Do not allow the mixture to become hot.

In a measuring jug, beat the egg lightly and add enough milk to make up to 125 ml/4 fl oz. Add the melted mixture to the dry ingredients with the beaten egg and milk mixture. Stir thoroughly; the mixture should run easily off the spoon.

Pour into the prepared tin and bake for 1¼–1½ hours until firm to the touch. Cool on a wire rack.

MAKES 1 (15 CM/6 INCH) SQUARE CAKE

HARVEST CAKE

A rich fruit cake is the basis for this autumn gift, but a plain Madeira cake can be used if preferred. The basket weave piping is done in royal icing; however buttercream can be used instead. The centre of the basket is filled with a selection of moulded marzipan fruits, vegetables and leaves.

500 g/1 lb 2 oz currants
250 g/9 oz raisins • 250 g/9 oz sultanas
250 g/9 oz butter, softened
250 g/9 oz moist dark brown sugar
grated rind of 1 lemon
65 g/2½ oz almonds, shelled
65 g/2½ oz citrus peel, chopped
90 g/3½ oz glacé cherries
250 g/9 oz plain flour
5 ml/1 tsp ground mixed spice
4 eggs, beaten
15 ml/1 tbsp black treacle

DECORATION

apricot jam, warmed and sieved
900 g/2 lb marzipan or almond paste
a little vodka or gin
900 g/2 lb sugar paste
450 g/1 lb Royal Icing (page 52), tinted with yellow
or cream food colouring
marzipan fruits, vegetable and leaves (page 87)

Set the oven at 150°C/300°F/gas 2. Line and grease a 23 cm/9 inch round cake tin.

Mix the currants, raisins and sultanas. Cream the butter with the sugar and lemon rind until very soft. Beat in the almonds and the citrus peel. Wash and dry the cherries, then roughly chop them and toss them with a little of the measured flour. Sift the remaining flour with the spice and toss a little with the mixed dried fruit. Beat the eggs and treacle into the creamed mixture, adding a spoonful of the flour occasionally to prevent the mixture from curdling. Fold in the remaining flour. Lastly fold in the fruit and the cherries.

Turn the mixture into the tin and smooth the top with the back of a wetted metal spoon, hollowing out the centre slightly. Cook for 4–5 hours. Insert a clean metal skewer into the centre of the cake to test if it is cooked: if it comes out clean, the cake is ready.

Leave the cake to cool in the tin for at least an hour, then transfer it to a wire rack to cool completely. Do not remove the lining paper. Wrap the cake, still in the lining paper, in fresh greaseproof paper and store it in an airtight tin until you are ready to ice it.

Brush the cake with sieved apricot jam and cover with marzipan or almond paste, then brush with vodka or gin and cover with sugar paste. To decorate the cake, centre it on a 28 cm/11 inch board. Cut out a 23 cm/9 inch circle of greaseproof paper and fold it in half. Draw a line parallel to the fold and 5 cm/2 inches away from it. Turn the paper over and draw another line 5 cm/2 inches from the fold. Open out the paper.

Place the pattern on top of the cake and mark the position of the two lines with a pin. Remove the pattern. Place some of the royal icing in an icing bag fitted with a basket nozzle and fill in the two end areas on top of the cake with basket weave piping. Fill a second piping bag, fitted with a writing nozzle, with royal icing and neaten the straight edges of the basket weave piping with a line of plain piping.

Pipe basket weave around the side of the cake. Finally, place the remaining royal icing in an icing bag fitted with a shell nozzle; neaten the top and bottom edges with a row of fine shells. Leave the icing to dry.

Arrange the fruits, vegetables and leaves down the centre of the cake.

YIELDS ABOUT 30 PORTIONS.

MRS BEETON'S TIP

For a simple Harvest Cake, follow the recipe above, but do not apply the covering of basket weave piping. Tie a wide gold ribbon around the cake and tie it in a flamboyant bow. Pinch the top edge of the marzipan or mark it decoratively with a fork. Top the cake with a generous arrangement of candied and crystallised fruit, such as pineapple, ginger, marrons glacés, glacé cherries and angelica.

BASKET WEAVE PIPING

This design can be piped in buttercream over a sponge cake, but the royal icing gives a neater effect. Allow plenty of time to pipe this design. The icing should be of a medium-peak consistency. For the best effect, use coloured icing. You will need a no 2 plain writing nozzle for the vertical lines and a basket or serrated ribbon nozzle for the horizontal piping. Have both nozzles fitted in separate bags of icing ready before you begin.

The design is often piped on the sides of the cake, so raise the cake so that it is at eye level by placing it on a turntable or cake tin. Sit down for steady, controlled piping.

Start at the back of the cake with the serrated nozzle and pipe a single 2.5 cm/1 inch long ribbon horizontally on the side of the cake at the top edge. Leave a gap the same width as the ribbon and pipe another ribbon underneath the first, beginning and ending at the same place. Repeat, leaving a gap between each ribbon until you reach the base of the cake.

Using the icing bag fitted with the plain nozzle, pipe a vertical line down the cake at the point where the ribbons end.

Using the serrated nozzle, pipe a second row of 2.5 cm/1 inch long ribbons over the vertical line and in between the first line of ribbons. Begin piping each ribbon parallel to the ribbon above and halfway along it. Pipe another vertical line with the plain nozzle. Continue in this way all around the cake to build up the pattern.

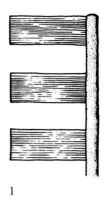

1

2

MRS BEETON'S TIP

Alternatively, the basket weave piping can be worked in horizontal rows. To do this, pipe a line of 2.5 cm/1 inch ribbons, with a space between each, all around the cake. Next pipe the vertical, straight lines, then pipe another horizontal row of ribbons underneath. Continue building up the pattern in this way.

3

Basket Weave Piping

ICED PETITS FOURS

fat for greasing
75 g/3 oz plain flour
2.5 ml/½ tsp salt
50 g/2 oz butter or margarine
3 eggs
75 g/3 oz caster sugar

FILLING AND DECORATION

jam, lemon curd or Buttercream (right),
using 50 g/2 oz butter
Glacé Icing (opposite)
food colouring (optional)
crystallized violets • silver balls
glacé fruits • angelica
chopped nuts

Line and grease a 25 × 15 cm/10 × 6 inch rectangular cake tin. Set the oven at 180°C/350°F/gas 4.

Sift the flour and salt into a bowl and put in a warm place. Melt the butter or margarine without letting it get hot. Set aside.

Whisk the eggs lightly in a mixing bowl. Add the sugar and place the bowl over a saucepan of hot water. Whisk for 10–15 minutes until thick. Take care that the bottom of the bowl does not touch the water. Remove from the heat and continue whisking until at blood-heat. The melted butter or margarine should be at the same temperature.

Sift half the flour over the eggs, then pour in half the melted butter or margarine in a thin stream. Fold in gently. Repeat, using the remaining flour and fat. Spoon gently into the prepared tin. Bake for 30–40 minutes. Cool on a wire rack.

Cut the cold cake in half horizontally, spread with the chosen filling and sandwich together again. Cut the cake into small rounds, triangles or squares and place on a wire rack set over a large dish. Brush off any loose crumbs.

Make up the icing to a coating consistency which will flow easily. Tint part of it with food colouring, if wished. Using a small spoon, coat the tops and sides of the cakes with the icing, or if preferred, pour it over the cakes, making sure that the sides are coated evenly all over. Decorate the tops of the cakes and leave to set. The cakes may be placed in paper cases for packing, if liked.

MAKES 18 TO 24

ROYAL ICING

It is vital to ensure that the bowl is clean and free from grease. A heavy-duty electric mixer is essential for making good royal icing, as beating by hand is extremely hard work and it is very difficult to achieve the correct light consistency. Using royal icing mix is an excellent alternative to making the icing from scratch as it avoids the use of raw egg; however, icing made from the packet mix also needs thorough beating.

2 egg whites
450 g/1 lb icing sugar, sifted
2.5 ml/½ teaspoon glycerine

Place the egg whites in a bowl and whisk them very lightly, just sufficiently to break them up. Gradually beat in about two-thirds of the icing sugar and continue beating until the icing is pure white and forms soft peaks. Then gradually add the remaining icing sugar and glycerine. The icing must not be too stiff.

Transfer the icing to an airtight container, cover the surface of the icing with cling film before putting the lid on the container. Before use, lightly beat the icing.

SUFFICIENT TO COAT THE TOP AND SIDES
OF 1 (20 CM/8 INCH) CAKE

BUTTERCREAM

100 g/4 oz butter, softened
15 ml/1 tbsp milk or fruit juice
225 g/8 oz icing sugar, sifted

In a mixing bowl, cream the butter with the milk or juice and gradually work in the icing sugar. Beat the icing until light and fluffy. Alternatively, work all the ingredients in a food processor, removing the plunger for the final mixing to allow air to enter the buttercream mixture.

SUFFICIENT TO FILL AND COAT THE TOP
OF 1 (20 CM/8 INCH) CAKE

GLACE ICING

This simple, basic icing is quickly prepared and is ideal for topping a plain sponge cake or a batch of small cakes. Make the icing just before it is to be used and keep any extra decorations to the minimum.

100 g/4 oz icing sugar, sifted
food colouring, optional

Place the icing sugar in a bowl. Using a wooden spoon gradually stir in sufficient warm water (about 15 ml/ 1 tbsp) to create icing whose consistency will thickly coat the back of the spoon. Take care not to add too much liquid or the icing will be too runny. At first the icing will seem quite stiff, but it will slacken rapidly as the icing sugar absorbs the water. Stir in 1–2 drops of food colouring, if required.

SUFFICIENT TO COVER THE TOP
OF 1 (18 CM/7 INCH) CAKE

VARIATIONS

Lemon or Orange Glacé Icing Use 15 ml/1 tbsp strained lemon or orange juice instead of the water.
Coffee Glacé Icing Dissolve 5 ml/1 tsp instant coffee in 15 ml/1 tbsp warm water and add instead of the water in the main recipe.
Liqueur-flavoured Glacé Icing Replace half the water with the liqueur of your choice.

CHOCOLATE GLACE ICING

An icing that contains dessert chocolate and/or butter will thicken and set more readily than one which merely contains a liquid.

50 g/2 oz plain chocolate, broken into small pieces
knob of butter
100 g/4 oz icing sugar, sifted

Combine the chocolate and butter in a heatproof bowl. Add 15 ml/1 tbsp water. Place the bowl over hot water. When the chocolate has melted, stir the mixture, then gradually add the sugar. Add a little more water, if necessary, to give a smooth coating consistency. Use the icing at once.

SUFFICIENT TO COAT THE TOP
OF 1 (18 CM/7 INCH) CAKE

MICROWAVE TIP

Melt the chocolate, butter and water in a bowl on Medium for 1–2 minutes.

A Choice of Biscuits

Shortbread is one of the favourite foods to bake and give, and Mrs Beeton's recipe, with its caraway seeds and topping of candied peel, is a real treat. There are dainty alternatives to shortbread and many are quite simple to make. If you are looking for a savoury gift rather than a sweet one, home-made oatcakes or old-fashioned crackers are the ideal choice, especially when packed with a generous wedge of Farmhouse Cheddar or a cheese local to the area where you live.

SHORTBREAD

Illustrated on page 26

fat for greasing
100 g/4 oz plain flour
1.25 ml/¼ tsp salt
50 g/2 oz rice flour, ground rice or semolina
50 g/2 oz caster sugar
100 g/4 oz butter

Invert a baking sheet, then grease the surface now uppermost. Set the oven at 180°C/350°F/gas 4.

Mix all the ingredients in a mixing bowl. Rub in the butter until the mixture binds together to a dough. Shape into a large round about 1 cm/½ inch thick. Pinch up the edges to decorate. Place on the prepared baking sheet, and prick with a fork. Bake for 40–45 minutes. Cut into wedges while still warm.

MAKES 8 WEDGES

VARIATION

Shortbread Biscuits Roll out the dough on a lightly floured surface to a thickness of just under 1 cm/½ inch. Cut into rounds with a 5–6 cm/2–2½ inch cutter. Place on 1–2 greased baking sheets, allowing room for spreading. Prick the surface of each biscuit in several places with a fork. Bake for 15–20 minutes. Leave to stand for a few minutes, then cool on a wire rack.

MELTING MOMENTS

fat for greasing
100 g/4 oz butter or margarine
75 g/3 oz caster sugar
30 ml/2 tbsp beaten egg
125 g/4½ oz self-raising flour
pinch of salt
rolled oats for coating
4–5 glacé cherries, quartered

Grease two baking sheets. Set the oven at 180°C/350°F/gas 4.

In a mixing bowl, cream the margarine or mixed fats and sugar until pale and fluffy. Add the egg with a little flour and beat again. Stir in the remaining flour with the salt, mix well, then shape the mixture into 16–20 balls with the hands.

Place the rolled oats on a sheet of greaseproof paper and toss the balls in them to coat them evenly all over. Space the balls on the prepared baking sheets. Place a small piece of glacé cherry in the centre of each.

Bake for about 20 minutes until pale golden brown. Leave to stand for a few minutes on the baking sheets, then cool on a wire rack.

MAKES 16 TO 20

VARIATION

Custard Treats Substitute 40 g/1½ oz of the flour with custard powder for a deliciously creamy biscuit with a rich butter colour. Omit the rolled oats coating.

FLORENTINES

oil for greasing
25 g/1 oz glacé cherries, chopped
100 g/4 oz cut mixed peel, finely chopped
50 g/2 oz flaked almonds
100 g/4 oz chopped almonds
25 g/1 oz sultanas
100 g/4 oz butter or margarine
100 g/4 oz caster sugar
30 ml/2 tbsp double cream
100 g/4 oz plain or couverture chocolate

Line 3 or 4 baking sheets with oiled greaseproof paper. Set the oven at 180°C/350°F/gas 4.

In a bowl, mix the cherries and mixed peel with the flaked and chopped almonds and the sultanas. Melt the butter or margarine in a small saucepan, add the sugar and boil for 1 minute. Remove from the heat and stir in the fruit and nuts. Whip the cream in a separate bowl, then fold it in.

Place small spoonfuls of the mixture on to the prepared baking sheets, leaving room for spreading. Bake for 8–10 minutes. After the biscuits have been cooking for about 5 minutes, neaten the edges by drawing them together with a plain biscuit cutter. Leave the cooked biscuits on the baking sheets to firm up slightly before transferring to a wire rack to cool completely.

To finish, melt the chocolate in a bowl over hot water and use to coat the flat underside of each biscuit. Mark into wavy lines with a fork as the chocolate cools.

MAKES 20 TO 24

BRANDY SNAPS

Brandy snaps filled with whipped cream are one of life's little luxuries. Pack the unfilled snaps carefully and include a tub of double cream as part of the present.

fat for greasing
50 g/2 oz plain flour
5 ml/1 tsp ground ginger
50 g/2 oz margarine
50 g/2 oz soft dark brown sugar
30 ml/2 tbsp golden syrup
10 ml/2 tsp grated lemon rind
5 ml/1 tsp lemon juice

Grease two or three 20 × 25 cm/8 × 10 inch baking sheets. Also grease the handles of several wooden spoons, standing them upside down in a jar until required. Set the oven at 180°C/350°F/gas 4.

Sift the flour and ginger into a bowl. Melt the margarine in a saucepan. Add the sugar and syrup and warm gently, but do not allow to become hot. Remove from the heat and add the sifted ingredients with the lemon rind and juice. Mix well.

Put small spoonfuls of the mixture on to the prepared baking sheets, spacing well apart to allow for spreading. Do not put more than 6 spoonfuls on a baking sheet. Bake for 8–10 minutes.

Remove from the oven and leave to cool for a few seconds until the edges begin to firm. Lift one of the biscuits with a palette knife and roll loosely around the greased handle of one of the wooden spoons. Allow to cool before removing the spoon handle. Repeat with the remaining biscuits.

MAKES 14 TO 18

ALMOND MACAROONS

fat for greasing
2 egg whites
150 g/5 oz caster sugar
100 g/4 oz ground almonds
10 ml/2 tsp ground rice
split almonds or halved glacé cherries

Grease 2 baking sheets and cover with rice paper. Set the oven at 160°C/325°F/gas 3.

In a clean dry bowl, whisk the egg whites until frothy but not stiff enough to form peaks. Stir in the sugar, ground almonds, and ground rice. Beat with a wooden spoon until thick and white.

Put small spoonfuls of the mixture 5 cm/2 inches apart on the prepared baking sheets or pipe them on. Place a split almond or halved glacé cherry on each macaroon and bake for 20 minutes or until pale fawn in colour. Cool slightly on the baking sheets, then finish cooling on wire racks.

MAKES 16 TO 20

VARIATION

Ratafias Ratafias are used in trifles, to decorate desserts, and as petits fours. Follow the recipe above, but reduce the size of the biscuits so that when cooked they are only 2 cm/$\frac{3}{4}$ inch in diameter. Omit the split almond or cherry topping.

CINNAMON STARS

Edible Christmas tree decorations make excellent gifts. Buy a biscuit tin with a festive design, or cover a box with festive wrapping paper, pack it with Cinnamon Stars and Snowmen (opposite) and present it with the proviso that it be opened before Christmas so that the contents can be hung on the tree.

fat for greasing
350 g/12 oz plain flour
5 ml/ 1 tsp bicarbonate of soda
10 ml/2 tsp ground cinnamon
2.5 ml/$\frac{1}{2}$ tsp ground ginger
150 g/5 oz butter
100 g/4 oz sugar
100 g/4 oz honey
1 egg yolk
30 ml/2 tbsp milk
flour for rolling out
150 g/5 oz dark chocolate, broken into squares, to decorate

Thoroughly grease 3–4 baking sheets. Set the oven at 180°C/350°F/gas 4. Mix the flour, bicarbonate of soda and spices in a bowl.

In a mixing bowl, beat the butter until soft, add the sugar and continue to beat until light and fluffy. Beat in the honey and egg yolk, then the milk. Fold in the flour mixture to make a dough.

Knead the biscuit dough lightly on a floured surface, then roll out to a thickness of 3 mm/$\frac{1}{8}$ inch. Cut into stars with a 5 cm/2 inch star-shaped biscuit cutter. Using a straw, make a small hole in each star. The hole should be on a point, but not too near the edge. Transfer the biscuits to the prepared baking sheets.

Bake for about 8 minutes, until golden brown. Cool for a few minutes, then transfer to wire racks.

Melt the chocolate with 15 ml/1 tbsp water in a saucepan over low heat. Brush the tips of each star generously with chocolate, then place on a wire rack until the chocolate has set. This process may be speeded up if the biscuits are chilled in the refrigerator.

When the chocolate is firm, thread a length of ribbon through each biscuit for hanging on the tree.

MAKES ABOUT 60

SNOWMEN

To make these American favourites you will require a snowman template: on a piece of heavy cardboard, arrange a 7.5 cm/3 inch biscuit cutter with a 5 cm/2 inch cutter on top to make a snowman shape. Draw round the shape, overlapping the cutters slightly to give a wide neck, and adding a top hat if liked. Cut out the template.

fat for greasing
225 g/8 oz plain flour • 45 ml/3 tbsp cocoa
5 ml/1 tsp bicarbonate of soda • 50 g/2 oz margarine
100 g/4 oz golden syrup
75 g/3 oz soft light brown sugar
1 egg, beaten

DECORATION

white Glacé Icing (page 53)
chocolate chips • glacé cherries
jelly diamonds
chocolate Glacé Icing (page 53) (optional)

Grease 3–4 baking sheets. Set the oven at 180°C/350°F/gas 4. Mix the flour, cocoa and bicarbonate of soda in a mixing bowl. Melt the margarine in a large saucepan. Add the syrup and sugar and warm gently, but do not allow to become hot. Remove from the heat.

Add the melted mixture to the dry ingredients with the beaten egg, and mix to a dough. Wrap in cling film and refrigerate for 1–2 hours.

Roll out the dough on a floured surface to a thickness of 5 mm/¼ inch. Using the template and a sharp knife, carefully cut out snowmen, re-rolling and re-cutting any trimmings. Use a straw to make a small hole in each snowman, near the top of the head or hat.

Transfer the snowmen to the prepared baking sheets and bake for 12–15 minutes until firm to the touch. Cool the biscuits on the baking sheets for a few minutes, then transfer them carefully to wire racks.

When cold, thread a length of fine string or thick cotton through each snowman. Ice each with white glacé icing and decorate as appropriate, using chocolate chips for eyes and small pieces of glacé cherry for mouths. Jelly diamonds make excellent coat buttons.

MAKES ABOUT 8

OATCAKES

Illustrated on page 23

A basket containing a little bottle of whisky, a tin of Oatcakes and some home-made Shortbread (page 54) would make a perfect themed present, particularly if you decorate the top of the gift with a few sprigs of heather.

fat for greasing
25 g/1 oz bacon fat or dripping
225 g/8 oz medium oatmeal
1.25 ml/¼ tsp salt
1.25 ml/¼ tsp bicarbonate of soda
fine oatmeal for rolling out

Grease 2 baking sheets. Set the oven at 160°C/325°F/gas 3.

Melt the bacon fat or dripping in a large saucepan. Remove from the heat and stir in the dry ingredients, then add 60–75 ml/4–5 tbsp boiling water to make a stiff dough.

When cool enough to handle, knead the dough well, then cut it in half. Roll out one piece on a surface dusted with fine oatmeal, to an 18 cm/7 inch circle. Cut into wedge-shaped pieces and transfer to the prepared baking sheets. Repeat with the remaining dough. Bake for 20–30 minutes. Cool on a wire rack.

MAKES ABOUT 16

MRS BEETON'S TIP

Children love to decorate Snowmen and other iced biscuits. Let them loose with a tub each of glacé cherries, jelly diamonds, sugar strands, chocolate chips and chocolate vermicelli and they will be happy for hours.

CHEESE STRAWS

fat for greasing
100 g/4 oz plain flour
pinch of mustard powder
pinch of salt
pinch of cayenne pepper
75 g/3 oz butter
75 g/3 oz grated Parmesan cheese
1 egg yolk
flour for rolling out

Grease 4 baking sheets. Set the oven at 200°C/400°F/ gas 6.

Sift the flour, mustard, salt and cayenne into a bowl. In a mixing bowl, cream the butter until soft and white, then add the flour mixture with the cheese. Stir in the egg yolk and enough cold water to form a stiff dough.

Roll out on a lightly floured surface to a thickness of about 5 mm/¼ inch and cut into fingers, each measuring about 10 × 1 cm/4 × ½ inch. From the pastry trimmings make several rings, each about 4 cm/1½ inches across.

With a palette knife, transfer both rings and straws to the prepared baking sheets and bake for 8–10 minutes or until lightly browned and crisp. Cool on the baking sheets.

To serve, fit a few straws through each ring and lay the bundles in the centre of a plate with any remaining straws criss-crossed around them.

MAKES 48 TO 60

MRS BEETON'S TIP

For a decorative effect, the straws may be twisted, corkscrew-fashion.

CHEESE BUTTERFLIES

A plateful of these tasty savouries would make a good contribution to a cocktail party.

fat for greasing
100 g/4 oz plain flour
pinch of mustard powder
pinch of salt
pinch of cayenne pepper
75 g/3 oz butter
75 g/3 oz grated Parmesan cheese
1 egg yolk
flour for rolling out

TOPPING
100 g/4 oz full-fat soft cheese
few drops of anchovy essence
few drops of red food colouring

Grease 2 baking sheets. Set the oven at 200°C/400°F/ gas 6. Sift the flour, mustard, salt and cayenne into a bowl. In a mixing bowl, cream the butter until soft and white, then add the flour mixture with the cheese. Stir in the egg yolk and enough cold water to form a stiff dough.

Roll out on a lightly floured surface to a thickness of about 3 mm/⅛ inch and cut into rounds about 6 cm/ 2½ inches in diameter. Cut half the rounds across the centre to make 'wings'.

With a palette knife, lift both the whole rounds and the 'wings' on to the prepared baking sheets and bake for 10 minutes. Cool on the baking sheets.

Meanwhile make the topping. Put the soft cheese in a bowl and cream until soft with a fork, adding the anchovy essence for flavour and just enough of the red food colouring to tint the mixture a pale pink. Transfer the topping to a piping bag fitted with a shell nozzle.

When the biscuits are quite cold, pipe a line of cheese across the centre of each full round and press the straight edges of two half-rounds into the cheese to make them stand up like wings.

MAKES 12 TO 18

HOT PEPPER CHEESES

When freshly cooked, these savouries are inclined to crumble and break easily. For this reason it is best to allow them to cool completely, pack them carefully in a rigid box or tin, and add a note with the suggestion that they be reheated gently and served warm.

fat for greasing
200 g/7 oz plain flour
200 g/7 oz butter
200 g/7 oz Lancashire cheese, grated
few drops of hot pepper sauce
1.25 ml/$\frac{1}{4}$ tsp salt
flour for rolling out

Grease 4 baking sheets. Sift the flour into a mixing bowl. Rub in the butter until the mixture resembles fine breadcrumbs. Add the cheese and seasonings. Work the mixture thoroughly by hand to make a smooth dough. Use a few drops of water if necessary, but the dough will be shorter and richer without it. Chill for 30 minutes.

Meanwhile, set the oven at 180°C/350°F/gas 4. Roll out the dough on a floured surface to a thickness of 5 mm/$\frac{1}{4}$ inch. Cut into rounds or shapes.

With a palette knife, transfer the shapes to the prepared baking sheets and bake for 10–12 minutes or until lightly browned and crisp. Cool on the baking sheets.

MAKES 40 TO 50

MRS BEETON'S TIP

When cutting out the cheese dough it is best to stick to regular shapes such as rounds, crescents, squares or stars. The mixture is so short that any thin projections on the biscuits are likely to break off.

CHESHIRE CHIPS

fat for greasing
50 g/2 oz plain flour
50 g/2 oz butter
50 g/2 oz Cheshire cheese, grated
50 g/2 oz soft white breadcrumbs
1.25 ml/$\frac{1}{4}$ tsp cayenne pepper
1.25 ml/$\frac{1}{4}$ tsp salt

Grease 4 baking sheets. Sift the flour into a mixing bowl. Rub in the butter until the mixture resembles fine breadcrumbs. Add the cheese, breadcrumbs and seasonings. Work the mixture thoroughly by hand to make a smooth dough. Chill for 30 minutes.

Meanwhile, set the oven at 180°C/350°F/gas 4. Roll out the dough on a floured surface to a thickness of 5 mm/$\frac{1}{4}$ inch. Cut into thin chips, each measuring about 3 mm × 5 cm/$\frac{1}{8}$ inch × 2 inches.

With a palette knife, transfer the chips to the prepared baking sheets and bake for 7–10 minutes. Cool.

MAKES 48 TO 60

CARAWAY CRACKERS
Illustrated on page 23

fat for greasing
50 g/2 oz butter
225 g/8 oz plain flour
30 ml/2 tbsp caraway seeds
good pinch of salt
1 egg, beaten
milk to glaze

Grease 2 baking sheets. Set the oven at 180°C/350°F/gas 4. Place the butter in a small bowl and beat it until it is very soft. Gradually beat in the flour, caraway seeds and salt until the ingredients are thoroughly mixed.

Add the beaten egg and 30 ml/2 tbsp water , then mix well to make a firm dough. Knead the dough briefly on a floured surface, then roll it out thinly and cut out 5 cm/2 inch circles.

Place the crackers on the baking sheets and brush them with a little milk, then bake them for about 12–15 minutes. Transfer the crackers to a wire rack and cool.

MAKES ABOUT 30

– Gifts from the Pantry –

Candied and Crystallized Fruit

Shop-bought candied fruit is a succulent and expensive luxury but it can be made at home without great skill or special equipment. The main requirement is patience as the process takes about 15 minutes a day for 10–14 days. Any attempt to increase the strength of the syrup too quickly will result in tough, hardened, and shrivelled fruit. Sugar alone can be used for syrup making but the fruit's texture is better if part of the sugar is replaced by glucose. Powdered glucose weighs the same as sugar, but if using liquid glucose, increase the weight by one-fifth.

Use well-flavoured fruits, fresh or canned, for example, apricots, pineapple or large, juicy plums. Very soft fruits, such as raspberries, tend to disintegrate. Fresh fruit should be firm yet ripe. Good quality canned fruit can be used; it lacks some of the full fresh flavour, but the canning process gives a good texture for candying. Canned fruit does not require cooking and the process is quicker than for fresh fruit.

Processed fruit should be packed in waxed-paper lined cardboard boxes. Interleave layers of fruit with waxed paper. Store in a cool, dry place; well processed fruit will keep for several months in these conditions.

Fresh Fruit

Day 1 Prepare the fruit according to type, discarding stones and cores or peel. Prick small perfect crab-apples, apricots, fleshy plums or greengages several times to the centre with a stainless fork.

Cover the prepared fruit with boiling water and simmer gently until just tender, 10–15 minutes for firm fruits, only 3–4 minutes for tender fruits.

Overcooking at this stage makes the fruit squashy, while undercooking makes it dark and tough.

For each 450 g/1 lb fruit, make a syrup from 250 ml/8 fl oz poaching water, 50 g/2 oz sugar and 100 g/4 oz glucose. Alternatively, use 150 g/5 oz preserving sugar instead of sugar and glucose. Stir until the sugar has dissolved, then bring the syrup to the boil.

Drain the fruit and place it in a small bowl, then pour the boiling syrup over it. If there is not enough syrup to cover it, make up some more, using the same proportions. Cover with a plate to keep the fruit under the syrup and leave for 24 hours.

Day 2 Drain the syrup into a saucepan. Add 50 g/2 oz sugar for each original 250 ml/8 fl oz water. Bring to the boil, then pour the syrup over the fruit. Cover and leave as before.

Days 3–7 Repeat Day 2

Day 8 Drain the syrup into a saucepan. Add 75 g/3 oz sugar for every original 250 ml/8 fl oz water, heat and stir until dissolved. Add the drained fruit and boil for 3–4 minutes, then pour the fruit and syrup back into the bowl. This boiling makes the fruit plump. Leave for 48 hours.

Day 10 Repeat Day 8. When cooled, the resulting syrup should be of the consistency of fairly thick honey. If the syrup is still thin, repeat Day 8 again. Leave for 4 days.

Day 14 The fruit will keep in this heavy syrup for 2–3 weeks or for 2 months in a covered jar in the refrigerator. To complete the process, remove the fruit from the syrup. Do not pierce the fruit. Place it on a wire rack over a plate and allow to drain for a few minutes.

Put the rack into a very cool oven (not higher than 50°C/122°F). Use an oven thermometer to check the temperature and wedge the door ajar to prevent the temperature from increasing.

Candied fruit caramelizes easily and the flavour is then spoilt. Drying should take 3–6 hours if the heat is continuous; it may take 2–3 days if using residual heat on several occasions. Do not allow the metal rack to touch the hot sides of the oven as this will cause the wire to become too hot. Turn the fruit gently with a fork, until it is no longer sticky to handle.

Pack in cardboard boxes with waxed paper lining each box and separating the layers. Store in a dry, cool place and do not keep for many months as the succulence will be lost.

Candied fruit should have a dry surface. If it remains sticky, the final sugar concentration in the fruit is probably too low. Humid storage conditions should be avoided.

Candied Canned Fruit

Try pineapple rings or cubes, plums, peaches or halved apricots. Keep the sizes as uniform as possible. These quantities are for about 450 g/1 lb drained fruit.

Day 1 Put the drained fruit into a large bowl. Measure the syrup into a saucepan and make it up to 250 g/8 fl oz with water if necessary. Stir in 200 g/7 oz preserving sugar or 100 g/4 oz sugar and 100 g/4 oz glucose. Heat gently and stir until the sugar has dissolved. Bring to the boil, then pour the syrup over the fruit. If there is not enough syrup to cover the fruit, prepare some more by using 225 g/8 oz sugar to 200 ml/7 fl oz water. Keep the fruit under the syrup with a plate. Leave for 24 hours.

Day 2 Drain the fruit, dissolve 50 g/2 oz sugar in the syrup, bring to the boil and pour over the fruit. Leave for 24 hours.

Days 3–4 Repeat Day 2.

Day 5 Pour the syrup into a saucepan. Add 75 g/3 oz sugar, warm the syrup to dissolve the sugar, then add the fruit. Boil for 3–4 minutes. Replace in the bowl. Leave for 48 hours.

Day 7 Repeat Day 5 and let the fruit boil until a little syrup cooked on a plate has the consistency of thick honey. Leave to soak for 3–4 days. If the syrup seems thin, add a further 75 g/3 oz sugar, dissolve it and boil the syrup with the fruit for a further few minutes. Leave to soak for 3–4 days.

Day 11 Finish the fruit as when candying fresh fruit (Day 14).

Candied Angelica

Pick bright, tender stalks in April, cut off the root ends and leaves. Make a brine with 15 g/½ oz salt and 2 litres/3½ pints water; bring it to the boil. Soak the stalks in brine for 10 minutes. Rinse in cold water. Put in a pan of fresh boiling water and boil for 5–7 minutes. Drain. Scrape to remove the outer skin. Continue as for candying fresh fruit from Day 1.

Candied Peel

Use oranges, lemons or grapefruit. Scrub the fruit thoroughly. Halve and remove the pulp carefully to avoid damaging the peel. Boil the peel for 1 hour. Give grapefruit peel, which is bitter, several changes of water. Drain well, and continue as for candying fresh fruit from Day 1. It is customary to pour some glacé syrup into half peels to set.

CRYSTALLIZED FRUIT

Have some granulated sugar on a sheet of polythene, greaseproof paper or foil. Lift a piece of fruit on a fork, dip it quickly into boiling water, drain briefly, then roll it in the sugar until evenly coated.

Making a Glacé Finish

This gives a smooth, shiny finish. Over gentle heat, dissolve 450 g/1 lb granulated sugar in 150 ml/¼ pint water, then boil. Dip each fruit into boiling water for 20 seconds, then drain. Pour a little boiling syrup into a warm cup, quickly dip the fruit and place it on a wire rack. When all the fruit has been dipped, place the rack in an oven at a temperature not exceeding 50°C/122°F, and turn the fruit often to ensure even drying.

When the syrup in the small cup becomes

Preserves that are made for giving: Clementines in Vodka (page 80), Piccalilli (page 82), Apple Chutney (page 84) and Quick Candied Peel.

cloudy, it must be discarded and replaced from the saucepan, which must be kept hot (but not boiling) and closely covered.

QUICK CANDIED PEEL
Soak grapefruit or lemon peel overnight to extract some of the bitterness. Cut the peel into long strips, 5 mm/¼ inch wide. Put in a saucepan, cover with cold water and bring slowly to the boil. Drain, add fresh water and bring to the boil again. Drain, and repeat 3 more times. Weigh the cooled peel and place with an equal quantity of sugar in a pan.

Just cover with boiling water, and boil gently until the peel is tender and clear. Cool, strain from the syrup, and toss the peel in caster or granulated sugar on greaseproof paper. Spread out on a wire rack to dry for several hours. Roll again in sugar if at all stick. When quite dry, pack in covered jars, or boxes. Add a label recommending that the peel be used within 3–4 months.

Sweet Preserves

A pot of home-made jam, jelly or marmalade is always popular. At Christmas time make several different preserves and pot them in small jars ready for inclusion in hampers. Add one or two luxuries, such as Apricots in Brandy (page 80). When making preserves for presenting as gifts, it is particularly important to follow the basic rules to ensure the results are the best possible, with a good set and excellent keeping qualities.

The majority of sweet preserves may be roughly grouped into two categories: those that set and those that are runny. Jams, jellies and marmalades are all set preserves, whereas conserves have a syrupy texture. Mincemeat is a combination of ingredients preserved by combining uncooked dried fruits, sugar and alcohol. It is thick rather than set. A third category comprises butters and cheeses which are thickened by cooking. Fruit curd is not strictly speaking a preserve, but it is used in the same way as jams and is regarded as a related product.

Achieving a set

Three ingredients are essential for a good set – pectin, sugar and acid. When these are correctly balanced the mixture will set.

Pectin Naturally present in some fruit, this is the glue-like ingredient found in the cell walls of the fruit. It is extracted by cooking, a process which is assisted by the presence of acid.

Sugar Sugar is added in proportion, depending on the pectin content of the fruit, then dissolved and boiled down to the correct concentration for the production of a set.

Acid Some fruits contain acid, others with a low acid content require the addition of lemon juice for making a good preserve. Not only does this promote pectin extraction but it also helps to give the preserve a good colour and sparkle.

Ingredients

Fruit Fruit contains the maximum amount of pectin before it ripens; however in this state its flavour is not at its best. For a good preserve, the ideal is to use some fruit which is not quite ripe along with ripe fruit for flavour. Overripe fruit is not suitable for set preserves, although it may be used for butters and cheeses.

It is important to know or to check the pectin content of the fruit. Fruits with a low pectin content may be combined with others which have a high pectin content, ensuring that the preserve sets well.

Acid If the fruit does not have a good acid content, add lemon juice in the initial stages of cooking to assist in pectin extraction.

Sugar Sugar should be measured carefully: too much will cause the jam to be syrupy, not set; too little and the jam will require long boiling to give a set at all, making it dark and overcooked.

Any sugar can be used; however special preserving sugar gives the best results as the large crystals dissolve slowly and evenly, producing less scum and giving a sparkling preserve. This said, granulated sugar is probably the more frequently used type and it is perfectly acceptable. The practice of warming the sugar before adding it to the cooked fruit helps to make it dissolve evenly and quickly.

Special sugar with pectin and acid added in the correct proportions for setting should be used according to the manufacturer's instructions. The boiling time is usually significantly shorter than with traditional ingredients. This type of sugar is very useful with low-pectin fruits or with exotic fruits.

Pectin Bottled pectin is also available for use with fruits that do not contain a good natural supply. Again, this should be used exactly according to the manufacturer's instructions.

Alternatively, fruit with a good pectin content such as apples, redcurrants and gooseberries may be cooked to a purée and used to set preserves made with fruit which does not have enough pectin. The purée is known as pectin stock. The whole, washed fruit (trimmed of bad parts, stalks and leaves) should be cooked to a pulp with water, then strained through muslin. Pectin stock may be combined with fruit such as strawberries, cherries or rhubarb to make a set preserve.

Equipment

Cooking Pan Do not use aluminium, copper, uncoated iron or zinc pans as these metals react with the fruit, adding unwanted deposits to the preserve and, in some cases, spoiling both colour and flavour.

A stainless steel pan is best. Alternatively, a heavy, well-coated (unchipped) enamel pan may be used. Good-quality non-stick pans are also suitable for making preserves.

Although a covered pan is used for long cooking of fruit which needs tenderizing (particularly citrus fruit for marmalade), for boiling with sugar a wide open pan is best. The wider the pan, the larger the surface area of preserve and the more efficient will be the process of evaporating unwanted liquid to achieve a set. Whatever the shape of the pan, it is essential that it is large enough to hold both cooked fruit and sugar without being more than half to two-thirds full, so that the preserve does not boil over when it is brought to a full rolling boil.

Knife Use a stainless steel knife for cutting fruit. A carbon steel implement will react with the fruit, causing discoloration.

Sugar Thermometer This is invaluable for checking the temperature of the preserve.

Saucer For testing for set (not essential).

Jelly Bag and Stand For making jellies and jelly marmalades you need a jelly bag and stand to strain the cooked fruit. You also need a large bowl to collect the juice. If you do not have a stand you can improvise by tying the four corners of the jelly bag to the legs of an upturned traditional kitchen stool by means of elastic. Instead of a jelly bag a large, double-thick piece of muslin may be used.

Jars Use sturdy, heatproof jars that have been thoroughly cleaned, rinsed in hot water and dried. Unless they are exceedingly dirty or have food deposits, there is no need to sterilize jars. However they must be washed in very hot soapy water (use rubber gloves to withstand the heat), then rinsed in hot or boiling water. Turn the jars upside down on folded clean tea-towels placed on a baking sheet or in a roasting tin, then put in a warm oven about 15 minutes before use.

Alternatively, wash the jars in a dishwasher just before use and leave them undisturbed to avoid contamination. They will be hot and perfectly clean.

Jam Funnel A wide metal funnel which fits into jars and makes filling them far easier.

Small Jug For ladling the preserve into the jars.

Covers and Lids The surface of the preserve should be covered with discs or waxed paper. Airtight lids should be plastic-coated as bare metal will react with fruit acids in the jam and corrode. Cellophane discs may be used with elastic bands; they are not ideal for long-term storage but are useful under lids which may not be well coated in plastic.

Labels It is important to label each pot with the type of preserve and date.

Preparation Techniques

All fruit should be trimmed of bruised or bad parts, stalks and leaves. Then it should be prepared according to type – peeled, cored, stoned, cut up and so on. All these trimmings, including any pips, should be tied in a piece of scalded muslin and cooked with the fruit, as they contain valuable pectin.

Make sure you have enough clean and warm jars, covers and labels.

Cooking Techniques

The prepared fruit should be cooked with acid and a little water if necessary. Soft fruits and others that yield a good volume of juice need only a little water to prevent them from drying out in the first stages of heating. The fruit must initially be cooked until it is thoroughly softened, preferably in a covered pan to prevent excessive evaporation. It is at this stage that the pectin is extracted.

Undercooking not only results in tough pieces of fruit in the preserve but also in insufficient pectin for a good set.

Adding Sugar When the fruit is thoroughly cooked the sugar may be added. If possible warm the sugar first, then add it to the fruit. Keep the heat low and stir until all the sugar has dissolved completely. This is important – if the preserve boils before all the sugar has dissolved, the sugar may crystallize.

Boiling until Set Once the sugar has dissolved, the preserve should be brought to a full, or rolling boil, This must be maintained until setting point is reached. This rapid boiling concentrates the sugar to the level needed to balance with the pectin.

Skimming At the end of cooking any scum which has collected on the surface of the preserve should be removed with a metal spoon. Sometimes a small knob of butter is added to disperse this scum or any remaining scum which cannot be removed.

Removing Stones If fruit is not stoned before cooking, the stones may be removed with a slotted spoon or small sieve as the preserve boils.

Testing for Setting It is important to turn the heat off or take the pan off the heat when testing for setting. If the preserve continues to cook it may boil beyond the setting point, then it will not set.

Flake Test The least reliable. Lift a mixing spoon out of the preserve and allow the mixture to drip off it. When setting point is reached the preserve does not drip off cleanly but tends to fall off, leaving small drips of flakes building up on the edge of the spoon.

Sauce Test A reliable method: have a cold saucer ready in the refrigerator, spoon a little preserve on it and set it aside in a cool place for a few minutes. Push the sample of preserve with your finger; it should have formed a distinct skin which wrinkles. If the sample does not have a skin, the preserve will not set.

Temperature Test The best test: when the correct sugar concentration is reached the boiling preserve should achieve a temperature of 105°C/ 220°F. Do not let the temperature go any higher.

Potting

Before potting, warm the jars and spread clean tea-towels or paper on the surface where the jars will stand. Have ready a tea-towel to hold or steady the jars (an oven glove is too bulky) and a dry tea-towel or absorbent kitchen paper for wiping up any bad spills on the jars. Never wipe the sides of very hot jars with a damp dish cloth.

Most preserves should be put into jars as soon as they are cooked. The jars should be full but not overfilled. There should be just a small space below the rim of the jar to prevent the preserve from touching the lid. Cover the surface of the hot preserve immediately with a disc of waxed paper, wax-side down, then put on lids at once.

Preserves with pieces of fruit or rind which tend to float should be left to stand for 15 minutes after cooking and before potting. This allows the preserve to set just enough to hold the fruit or rind in position. The preserve should be stirred and potted, covered with waxed discs, then left to cool completely before covering with lids.

Storing

Store preserves in a cool, dark cupboard. They will keep from 6 to 12 months or longer in the right conditions. Since most modern homes now have central heating, preserves tend to dry out during storage by slow evaporation. This can be averted if the rims of lids are sealed with heavy freezer tape.

Basic Fruit Jams

To make a fruit jam you should know the pectin content. Fruits which have a good pectin content require an equal weight of sugar. Fruit with an excellent pectin content – currants, gooseberries or apples – can take up to one-and-a-quarter times their weight in sugar. Fruit with medium or poor pectin content will only set three-quarters of their weight in sugar. If the pectin content is poor, add pectin stock (page 63), plenty of lemon juice or commercial pectin.

Pectin Test

Place a little methylated spirits in a clean, old jar. Add a spoonful of the thoroughly cooked fruit pulp (before sugar is added) and gently swirl the mixture. Allow the pulp to settle. If it forms a large lump, the fruit has a good pectin content. If there are a few lumps, then the fruit has a moderate pectin content. If the pulp is separated in lots of small lumps, it has little pectin and more should be added for a good set. These lumps are known as clots. Discard jar and contents after testing.

Yield

Although it is possible to estimate the yield of most jams and many marmalades, jellies rely on the volume of juice which is extracted from the fruit for the weight of sugar which has to be added. In the recipes that follow, it has therefore not always been possible to estimate yields accurately.

MRS BEETON'S TIP

When making Plum and Apple Jam, or any stone fruit jam, clip a stone basket to the side of the preserving pan to hold the stones while allowing the juice to drip back into the pan. A metal sieve, hooked over one side of the pan and supported by the handle on the other, performs equally well.

APRICOT JAM

575 g/1¼ lb dried apricots
2 lemons
1.5 kg/3¾ lb sugar
50 g/2 oz flaked almonds

Wash the apricots and cut up each fruit in two or three pieces. Put them into a large bowl, cover the fruit with 1.5 litres/2¾ pints water and soak for 24 hours.

Transfer the fruit and soaking liquid to a preserving pan. Squeeze the juice from the lemons. Chop one lemon shell and tie it in scalded muslin. Add the juice and muslin bag to the apricots. Bring to the boil, lower the heat and simmer for about 30 minutes or until tender, stirring occasionally. Remove the muslin bag, squeezing it to extract all the juice.

Stir in the sugar and almonds. Stir over low heat until the sugar is dissolved, then bring to the boil. Boil rapidly until setting point is reached. Remove from the heat, skim, pot, cover and label.

MAKES ABOUT 2 KG/4½ LB

PLUM AND APPLE JAM

675 g/1½ lb apples
675 g/1½ lb plums
1.5 kg/3¾ lb sugar

Peel, core and slice the apples, Tie the trimmings in a piece of muslin. Wash the plums and put them into a preserving pan with the apples and the muslin bag. Add 450 ml/¾ pint water. Bring to the boil, then cook over gentle heat until the apples are pulpy and the skins of the plums are soft.

Add the sugar, stir over low heat until dissolved, then bring to the boil. Boil rapidly until setting point is reached. Use a slotted spoon to remove the plum stones as they rise to the surface (see Mrs Beeton's Tip). Remove from the heat, skim, pot, cover and label.

MAKES ABOUT 2.5 KG/5½ LB

BLACKBERRY AND APPLE JAM

450 g/1 lb sour apples
1 kg/2¼ lb blackberries
1.5 kg/3¼ lb sugar

Peel, core and slice the apples. Tie the trimmings in muslin. Put the apples and muslin bag in a saucepan, add 150 ml/¼ pint water and bring to the boil. Lower the heat and simmer the fruit until it forms a pulp.

Meanwhile, pick over the blackberries, wash them gently but thoroughly and put them in a second pan. Add 150 ml/¼ pint water, bring to the boil, then lower the heat and cook until tender.

Combine the fruits, with their cooking liquid, in a preserving pan. Add the sugar and stir over low heat until dissolved. Bring to the boil and boil rapidly until setting point is reached. Remove from the heat, skim, pot, cover and label.

MAKES ABOUT 2.5 KG/5½ LB

VARIATION

Seedless Blackberry and Apple Jam Make the apple purée and cook the blackberries as described in paragraphs 1 and 2 above, then rub through a fine nylon sieve set over a bowl to remove the seeds. Mix all the fruit together and weigh the mixture. Weigh out an equal quantity of sugar. Transfer the fruit to a preserving pan and simmer until thick. Add the sugar and stir over low heat until dissolved, then bring to the boil and boil rapidly until setting point is reached. Pot as suggested above.

MRS BEETON'S TIP

When making Quince Jam (right), if the quinces are very hard, they may be grated or minced coarsely, in which case the amount of water used should be doubled.

RASPBERRY CONSERVE

This conserve does not set firmly but it has a wonderful fresh flavour.

1.5 kg/3¼ lb sugar
1.25 g/2¾lb raspberries

Put the sugar in a heatproof bowl and warm in a preheated 150°C/300°F/gas 2 oven.

Meanwhile wash the raspberries lightly but thoroughly and drain them well. Put them in a preserving pan without any additional water, bring them gently to the boil, then boil rapidly for 5 minutes.

Draw the preserving pan off the heat and add the warmed sugar. Return the pan to the heat and stir well until all the sugar has dissolved. Bring to the boil and boil rapidly for 1 minute.

Remove from the heat, skim quickly, pot at once and label the conserve.

MAKES ABOUT 2.5 KG/5½ LB

QUINCE JAM

This jam has a delicious flavour but is rather solid, almost like a fruit cheese.

1.5 kg/3¼ lb quinces, peeled, cored and cut up (see Mrs Beeton's Tip)
juice of 1 large lemon
1.5 kg/3¼ lb sugar

Combine the quinces and lemon juice in a preserving pan. Add 250 ml/8 fl oz water, bring to the boil, then lower the heat and simmer until soft.

Add the sugar, stirring over low heat until dissolved. Bring to the boil and boil quickly until setting point is reached. Remove from the heat, skim, pot, cover and label the jam.

MAKES ABOUT 2.5 KG/5½ LB

WHOLE STRAWBERRY JAM

1.5 kg/3¼ lb strawberries, hulled
juice of 1 lemon
1.5 kg/3¼ lb sugar

Combine the strawberries and lemon juice in a preserving pan. Heat gently for 10 minutes, stirring all the time, to reduce the volume. Add the sugar, stirring over low heat until it has dissolved.

Bring to the boil and boil rapidly until setting point is reached. Remove from the heat and skim. Leave the jam undisturbed to cool for about 20 minutes or until a skin forms on the surface and the fruit sinks. Stir gently to distribute the strawberries. Pot and top with waxed paper discs. Cover and label when cold. Do not use twist-topped jars; the jam will have cooled down too much before potting.

MAKES ABOUT 2.5 KG/5½ LB

PEACH JAM

Citric acid and tartaric acid are available from chemists or shops which sell home-brewing and wine-making supplies.

1.8 kg/4 lb small firm peaches, peeled and quartered
(see Mrs Beeton's Tip)
5 ml/1 tsp citric or tartaric acid
1.5 kg/3¼ lb sugar

Combine the fruit, with the stones, and citric or tartaric acid in a preserving pan. Add 300 ml/½ pint water, bring to the boil, lower the heat and simmer until the fruit is tender.

Add the sugar and stir over gentle heat until dissolved. Bring to the boil and boil rapidly, removing the stones as they rise to the surface (see Mrs Beeton's Tip for Plum and Apple Jam, page 66). Test for set after about 10 minutes of rapid boiling.

When ready, remove from the heat, skim, pot, cover and label.

MAKES ABOUT 2.5 KG/5½ LB

GOOSEBERRY JAM

1.25 kg/2¾ lb gooseberries, topped and tailed
1.5 kg/3¼ lb sugar

Put the gooseberries in a preserving pan. Add 500 ml/17 fl oz water and bring to the boil. Lower the heat and simmer for 20–30 minutes, until the fruit is soft.

Add the sugar, stirring over gentle heat until dissolved. Bring to the boil and boil rapidly until setting point is reached. Test for set after about 10 minutes of rapid boiling. Remove from the heat, skim, pot, cover and label.

MAKES ABOUT 2.5 KG/5½ LB

DAMSON JAM

1.25 kg/2¾ lb damsons, stalks removed
1.5 kg/3¼ lb sugar
2.5 ml/½ tsp ground cloves
2.5 ml/½ tsp grated nutmeg

Put the damsons in a preserving pan with 500 ml/17 fl oz water. Place over gentle heat and cook for about 15 minutes, until the damsons are well broken down.

Add the sugar and spices and stir over gentle heat until dissolved. Bring to the boil and boil rapidly, removing the stones as they rise to the surface (see Mrs Beeton's Tip for Plum and Apple Jam, page 66). Test for set after about 10 minutes of rapid boiling. When ready, remove from the heat, skim, pot, cover and label.

MAKES ABOUT 2.5 KG/5½ LB

MRS BEETON'S TIP

To peel peaches, place them in a heatproof bowl, pour on boiling water to cover and leave for 30 seconds. Drain, cut a small cross in the top of each fruit and peel away the skin. Do this just before using the peaches, as they will discolour if allowed to stand.

GREENGAGE JAM

1.5 kg/3¼ lb greengages
1.5 kg/3¼ lb sugar

Remove the stalks, wash the greengages and put them into a preserving pan. Add 125 ml/4 fl oz water (see Mrs Beeton's Tip). Cook slowly for 5–20 minutes, until the fruit is broken down.

Add the sugar and stir over gentle heat until dissolved. Bring to the boil and boil rapidly, removing the stones as they rise to the surface (see Mrs Beeton's Tip for Plum and Apple Jam, page 66). Test for set after about 10 minutes of rapid boiling. When ready, remove from the heat, skim, pot, cover and label.

MAKES ABOUT 1.5 KG/3¼ LB

RAISIN PRESERVE

The fruit may be boiled for 1½ hours, or longer, for a sweet, dark fruit cheese. This lighter recipe, pepped up with rum, is good with pancakes or scones.

450 g/1 lb raisins
50 g/2 oz candied citron peel, chopped
10 ml/2 tsp ground cinnamon
1.25 ml/¼ tsp ground cloves
225 g/8 oz sugar
75 ml/3 fl oz rum

Mix the raisins and the citron peel in a large bowl. Add 150 ml/¼ pint water, the cinnamon, cloves and sugar. Mix well, then cover the bowl and leave to stand for 24 hours, stirring occasionally.

Tip the raisin mixture into a saucepan, scraping in all the juices from the bowl. Heat gently, stirring, until any remaining sugar has dissolved. Bring to the boil, lower the heat and cover the pan, then simmer steadily for 30 minutes. Mash the raisins with a potato masher to crush some of them. Stir in the rum, cover the pan again, then cook for a further 5 minutes. Stir well and pot, pressing the fruit down. Cover at once.

MAKES ABOUT 900 G/2 LB

MINT JELLY

Illustrated on page 72

1 kg/2¼ lb green apples
1 small bunch of mint
500 ml/17 fl oz distilled vinegar
sugar (see method)
20 ml/4 tsp finely chopped mint
green food colouring (optional)

Wash the apples, cut into quarters; put in a preserving pan with the small bunch of mint. Add 500 ml/17 fl oz water, bring to the boil, lower the heat and simmer until the apples are soft and pulpy. Add the vinegar, bring to the boil and boil for 5 minutes.

Strain through a scalded jelly bag and leave to drip for several hours or overnight (see page 64). Measure the juice and return it to the clean pan. Add 800 g/1¾ lb sugar for every 1 litre/1¾ pints of juice

Heat gently, stirring until the sugar has dissolved, then boil rapidly until close to setting point. Stir in the chopped mint, with colouring, if used, and boil steadily until setting point is reached. Remove from the heat, pot and cover immediately.

MRS BEETON'S TIP

When making Greengage Jam (above left) ripe or very juicy fruit will need very little water and only a short cooking time; firmer varieties may take as long as 20 minutes to break down and will need up to 250 ml/8 fl oz water.

CLEAR SHRED ORANGE MARMALADE

1.5 kg/3¼ lb Seville or bitter oranges
2 lemons
1 sweet orange
sugar (see method)

Wash the oranges and lemons. Squeeze the fruit and strain the juice into a large bowl. Reserve the fruit shells, pulp and pips.

Scrape all the pith from the shells and put it in a large bowl with the pulp and pips. Add 2 litres/3½ pints water and set aside. Shred the orange and lemon peel finely and add it to the bowl of juice. Stir in 2 litres/3½ pints water. Leave both mixtures to soak for 24 hours if liked.

Line a strainer with muslin and strain the liquid containing the pips into a preserving pan. Bring up the sides of the muslin and tie to make a bag containing the pith, pips and pulp. Add the bag to the pan, with the contents of the second bowl.

Bring the liquid to simmering point and simmer for 1½ hours or until the peel is tender. Remove from the heat. Squeeze the muslin bag between two plates over the pan to extract as much of the pectin-rich juice as possible (see Mrs Beeton's Tip).

Measure the liquid, return it to the pan and then add 800 g/1¾ lb sugar for every 1 litre/1¾ pints of juice. Heat gently until the sugar has dissolved, then bring to the boil and boil fast until setting point is reached. Remove from the heat and skim quickly.

Leave to cool slightly until a skin forms on the surface of the marmalade, then pot and top with waxed paper discs. Cover and label when cold.

MAKES ABOUT 4 KG/9 LB

VARIATION

Lemon Shred Marmalade Wash and peel 675 g/1½ lb lemons. Shred the peel finely, removing some of the pith if thick. Cut up the fruit, reserving the pips, pith and coarse tissue. Put the fruit and shredded peel in a large bowl with 1 litre/1¾ pints water. Put the pips, pith and coarse tissue from the lemons in a second bowl and add 1 litre/1¾ pints water. Proceed as in the recipe above, boiling the marmalade rapidly in the final stages for about 20 minutes until setting point is reached.

FIVE FRUIT MARMALADE

Illustrated on page 72

1 kg/2¼ lb fruit (1 orange, 1 grapefruit, 1 lemon,
1 large apple, 1 pear)
1.5 kg/3¼ lb sugar

Wash the citrus fruit, peel it and shred the peel finely. Scrape off the pith and chop the flesh roughly. Put the pips and pith in a bowl with 500 ml/17 fl oz water. Put the peel and chopped flesh in a second, larger bowl with 1.5 litres/2¾ pints water. Leave both mixtures to soak for 24 hours if liked.

Line a strainer with muslin and strain the liquid containing the pips into a preserving pan. Bring up the sides of the muslin and tie to make a bag containing the pith and pips. Add the bag to the pan, with the contents of the second bowl. Peel and dice the apple and pear and add to the pan.

Bring the liquid to the boil, lower the heat and simmer for 1¼ hours or until the volume is reduced by one-third. Remove from the heat. Squeeze the muslin bag over the pan to extract as much of the pectin-rich juice as possible.

Return the pan to the heat, add the sugar and stir over low heat until dissolved. Bring to the boil and boil rapidly for about 30 minutes or until setting point is reached. Remove from the heat and skim quickly.

Leave to cool slightly until a skin forms on the surface of the marmalade, then stir, pot and top with waxed paper discs. Cover and label when cold.

MAKES ABOUT 2.5 KG/5½ LB

MRS BEETON'S TIP

If a very clear jelly is required, do not squeeze the muslin bag; instead tie it to the handle and allow the liquid to drip slowly back into the pan.

DARK COARSE-CUT MARMALADE
Illustrated on page 72

....

1.5 kg/3¼ lb Seville oranges
2 lemons
3 kg/6½ lb sugar
15 ml/1 tbsp black treacle

....

Wash the oranges and lemons. Squeeze the fruit and strain the juice into a preserving pan. Reserve the fruit shells, pulp and pips. Slice the peel into medium-thick shreds, then add it to the pan.

Scrape all the pith from the shells and tie it loosely in a muslin bag with the pulp and pips. Add to the preserving pan with 4.5 litres/8 pints water. Bring the liquid to simmering point and simmer for 1½–2 hours or until the peel is tender and the liquid has reduced by at least one third. Remove from the heat. Squeeze the muslin bag gently over the pan.

Add the sugar and treacle. Return to a low heat and stir until the sugar has dissolved, then bring to the boil and boil fast until setting point is reached. Remove from the heat and skim quickly.

Leave to cool slightly until a skin forms on the surface of the marmalade, then stir, pot, and top with waxed paper discs. Cover and label when cold.

MAKES ABOUT 5 KG/11 LB

....

MRS BEETON'S TIP

The quickest method of preparing fruit for marmalade is to opt for a chunky preserve, then simply wash and chop the whole fruit, discarding pips as you work.

KUMQUAT CONSERVE
Illustrated on page 72

....

Kumquats are closely related to citrus fruits; the name actually means 'gold orange'. Unlike oranges, however, they have thin edible rind and may be eaten whole. When buying kumquats, look for firm unblemished fruits with a rich aromatic smell.

....

575 g/1¼ lb kumquats
1 lemon
400 g/14 oz sugar

....

Slice the kumquats in half and remove the pips, setting them aside. Peel the lemon, then roughly chop the flesh, setting aside the pips and any coarse tissue or pith. Tie all the trimmings in a muslin bag and put the kumquats and lemon flesh in a large saucepan. Add the muslin bag and pour in 400 ml/14 fl oz water.

Bring to the boil, lower the heat, cover the pan and simmer for 30 minutes or until the kumquats feel tender when pierced with a skewer. Squeeze out the muslin bag over the pan.

Stir the sugar into the pan, trying not to break up the fruit. Cook gently, stirring until all the sugar has dissolved, then boil until setting point is reached.

Remove from the heat and skim quickly, if necessary. Leave to cool slightly until a skin forms on the surface of the conserve, then stir, pot and top with waxed paper discs. Cover and label when cold.

MAKES ABOUT 800 G/1¾ LB

....

ORANGE SHRED AND APPLE JELLY

Illustrated opposite

1 kg/2¼ lb crab-apples or windfalls
2 oranges
sugar (see method)

Wash the apples and cut into chunks, discarding any bruised or damaged portions. Place in a preserving pan with just enough water to cover. Bring to the boil, lower the heat and simmer for about 1 hour or until the fruit is tender. Strain through a scalded jelly bag, leaving it to drip for 1 hour.

Meanwhile wash the oranges. Squeeze and strain the juice, retaining the empty orange shells, Remove and discard the pith from each shell, then cut them in half. Put the quarters of peel into a small pan, add 100 ml/3½ fl oz water, cover and cook over gentle heat for 1 hour or until tender.

Strain the water used for cooking the orange peel into a large measuring jug. Add the apple extract and the orange juice. Weigh out 800 g/1¾ lb sugar for every 1 litre/1¾ pints of liquid.

Dry the cooked peel in a clean cloth and cut into fine shreds. Set aside.

Combine the liquid and sugar in the clean preserving pan. Heat gently until the sugar has dissolved, then bring to the boil and boil fast until setting point is reached. Remove from the heat and skim quickly. Add the reserved shreds of peel; do not stir.

Leave to cool slightly until a skin forms on the surface of the jelly, then pot and top with waxed paper discs. Cover and label when cold.

A selection of preserves for giving, including Mint Jelly (page 69), Kumquat Conserve (page 71), Orange Shred and Apple Jelly, Five Fruit Marmalade (page 70) and Dark Coarse-cut Marmalade (page 71).

MINCEMEAT

A pot of mincemeat is a welcome gift from visitors who call in the weeks running up to Christmas. As a Christmas present it is a little too late.

200 g/7 oz cut mixed peel
200 g/7 oz seedless raisins
25 g/1 oz preserved stem ginger
200 g/7 oz cooking apples
200 g/7 oz shredded suet
200 g/7 oz sultanas
200 g/7 oz currants
200 g/7 oz soft light brown sugar
50 g/2 oz chopped blanched almonds
generous pinch each of mixed spice, ground ginger
and ground cinnamon
grated rind and juice of 2 lemons and 1 orange
150 ml/¼ pint brandy, sherry or rum

Mince or finely chop the peel, raisins and ginger. Peel, core and grate the apples. Combine all the ingredients in a very large bowl, cover and leave to stand for 2 days in a cool place, stirring occasionally (see Mrs Beeton's Tip). Pot, cover and label. Store mincemeat in a cool, dry place.

MAKES ABOUT 1.8 KG/4 LB

VARIATIONS

Use a vegetarian 'suet' if you prefer a mincemeat free from animal products. If an alcohol-free mincemeat is desired, use apple juice instead of brandy and store the jars in the refrigerator if not using at once. Alternatively, freeze for up to 6 months.

MRS BEETON'S TIP

Observing the standing and stirring time helps to stop the mincemeat from fermenting later.

EXCELLENT MINCEMEAT

3 large cooking apples, cored
3 large lemons
450 g/1 lb raisins
450 g/1 lb currants
450 g/1 lb suet
900 g/2 lb soft light brown sugar
25 g/1 oz candied orange peel, chopped
25 g/1 oz candied citron or lemon peel, chopped
30 ml/2 tbsp orange marmalade
250 ml/8 fl oz brandy

Set the oven at 200°C/400°F/gas 6. Place the apples in an ovenproof dish, cover tightly and bake for 50–60 minutes, until thoroughly tender. Leave to cool.

Wash, dry and grate the lemons. Squeeze out the juice and reserve with the rind. Chop the shells, place them in a small saucepan and add cold water to cover. Bring to the boil, lower the heat and cover the pan. Simmer for about 1 hour, or until the shells are soft enough to chop very finely. Drain, cool and chop.

Scoop the apple flesh from the skins. Place it in a large bowl. Stir in the reserved lemon rind and juice with all the remaining ingredients. Cover the bowl and leave for 2 days, stirring occasionally. Pot, pressing the mincemeat down well. Cover tightly and store for at least 2 weeks before using.

MAKES ABOUT 4 KG/9 LB

LEMON CURD

Lemon curd is not a true preserve but it keeps for a while in the refrigerator. Use very fresh eggs bought from a reputable source.

2 lemons
225 g/8 oz lump or granulated sugar
75 g/3 oz butter, cut up
3 eggs

Wash, dry and grate the lemons. Squeeze out the juice and put it with the sugar in the top of a double saucepan or heatproof bowl set over boiling water. Stir occasionally until the sugar has dissolved. Remove from the heat and stir in the butter. Leave to cool.

Beat the eggs lightly in a bowl. Pour the cooled lemon mixture over them, mix well, then strain the mixture back into the pan or bowl. Place over gentle heat, stirring frequently until the mixture thickens enough to coat the back of a wooden spoon lightly. Pour into warmed clean jars. Cover with waxed paper discs. Put on lids and label when cold. Leave for 24 hours to thicken; store in the refrigerator. Use within 2–3 weeks.

MAKES ABOUT 450 G/1 LB

VARIATION

Orange Curd Substitute 2 oranges and add the juice of 1 lemon. Use only 50 g/2 oz butter, melting it in the double saucepan or bowl before adding the rind, juices and sugar.

Bottled Fruits and Syrups

Both bottled fruits and syrups make traditional and highly acceptable gifts. If you want to make a quick alternative, remember that fruit can be preserved in alcohol, such as brandy or vodka. Dried fruit bottled in vodka makes an interesting liqueur and a potent dessert; try apricots, peaches or mangoes.

BOTTLED FRUIT

For success and food safety, it is vital to follow the timings and instructions exactly when bottling fruit. Bottled fruit is preserved by heating. The fruit and liquid in the jar are heated to a high enough temperature, and for sufficient time, to kill micro-organisms (bacteria, yeasts and moulds). The jar must be sealed while the contents are at the high temperature to prevent any new micro-organisms from entering. Follow the recommended cooking method and timings exactly.

Before storing bottled fruit always check that each jar is sealed. Should you discover a reject jar within a day of the fruit being processed, transfer the fruit to a covered container, chill it and use it within two days, as you would fresh poached fruit. If you discover that the seal on bottled fruit is gone some time after it has been stored, discard the contents in case they have been contaminated with organisms that may cause food poisoning.

Similarly, if you find that fruit is fermenting or that it looks or tastes strange, discard it for safety's sake.

Equipment

Preserving Jars Special preserving jars must be used for bottled fruit. They are manufactured to withstand the high temperatures and to form an airtight seal when the contents are processed correctly. The jars must be in good condition; any that are chipped, cracked or damaged in any way will not seal properly even if they do withstand the temperature during processing.

There are two types of preserving jars: screw band jars or clip jars. Screw bands, made of metal or plastic, usually have a built-in rubber (or plastic) ring which provides the seal. New screw bands should be loosened by a quarter turn before processing to allow for expansion when heated.

Clip jars have metal clips and separate rubber rings to seal the lids. The rubber rings should be replaced each time they are used, otherwise they will not seal the jar properly. Old, unused rubber rings should not be used as they tend to perish during prolonged storage. The metal clips expand slightly as they are heated so these jars are sealed before processing.

Saucepan and Stand The fruit may be processed in the oven or in a saucepan. The saucepan must be deep enough to submerge the jars or bottles in water. The bottles must be placed on a stand in the base of the saucepan. Slats of wood may be placed in the bottom of the saucepan or a thick pad of newspaper may be used as a stand for the jars.

Oven Method If the fruit is processed in the oven, the jars are placed on a thick pad of newspaper in a roasting tin.

Tongs, Thermometer, Oven Glove and Wooden Board Special preserving tongs are best for lifting the hot jars out of a saucepan; they are also useful for lifting jars processed in the oven. A thermometer should be used to check the temperature of the water when processing. An oven glove is essential for holding the jars and a clean, dry wooden board must be used as a stand for hot jars. Hot jars that are placed on a cold or damp surface will crack.

Preparing the Jars

The jars must be spotlessly clean. They should be washed in hot, soapy water, rinsed in hot or boiling water and allowed to drain upside down on clean tea-towels. The jars should be left upside down to drain until they are filled.

If the jars are particularly dirty (for example if they have been stored for some time) they should be sterilized. Sterilized jars should be used for any fruits that are packed in brandy or other spirit without being processed. To sterilize jars, first wash them in hot soapy water, rinse them, then stand them on

slats of wood, a rack or a pad of paper in a deep pan. Pour in cold water to cover the jars completely. Put any lids, clips and rings into the pan. Heat gently until the water boils, then boil the jars for 5 minutes. Turn the heat off and leave the jars submerged until they are to be used, when they should be drained upside down on clean tea-towels spread on a work surface. Alternatively, sterilizing products for wine-making may be used to sterilize jars.

Liquid for Bottling

Fruit is usually bottled in syrup; however, fruit juice may be used instead. The syrup may be combined with brandy or other spirits or liqueurs, or it may be flavoured with spices, such as cinnamon sticks or cloves. Strips of orange or lemon rind may also be used to flavour the syrup.

Syrup There is no rule about the quantity of sugar used in a syrup for bottling. Heavy syrups tend to make the fruit rise in the jar, which spoils the appearance of the preserve (only a problem if the bottled fruit is prepared for a competition or exhibition). Brown sugar may be used if preferred but the fruit will take on the dark colour. Honey may also be used to sweeten the bottling liquid. The following is a guide to quantities of sugar to add to 1 litre/1¾ pints of water when making syrup.

   light syrup: 200 g/7 oz sugar (for apples)
   medium syrup: 400–575 g/14 oz–1¼ lb sugar (for all fruit)
   heavy syrup: 800 g/1¾ lb sugar (for peaches)

Dissolve the sugar in the water, bring to the boil and boil for 2 minutes. Remove from the heat and cover the pan to prevent any extra water from evaporating.

Preparing the Fruit

Only bottle perfectly fresh, prime-quality fruit. Wash, dry and trim the fruit, then cut it into even-sized pieces if necessary. Avoid over-handling the fruit. Soft fruits, in particular, should be handled as little as possible to avoid bruising or spoiling them.

Mince Pies and Brandy Butter (both on page 37) are the ideal combination for a simple Christmas offering.

Scald a wooden spoon and use its handle to ease the fruit into position when packing the jars. The fruit should be closely packed but not squashed. Apples may be solid packed, leaving little air space or room for syrup.

Apples Peel, core and cut into 5 mm/¼ inch thick slices or rings. As the apples are prepared, put them into brine to prevent discoloration. Drain and rinse well, then dry before packing. For solid packs, blanch apples in boiling water for 2 minutes, drain and pack.

Apricots Ripe, not soft, apricots may be bottled whole or halved with stones removed. Crack some stones and add a few kernels to jars of halved fruit.

Blackberries Select large, fully ripe fruit.

Cherries Select plump fruit with small stones. Morello cherries are best. Remove stalks. Stone fruit if liked, reserving all juice to add to syrup.

Currants (black, red or white) Select large, ripe fruit. String and pack in jars. Redcurrants and whitecurrants have large seeds and are best mixed with raspberries.

Damsons Remove stalks. Wipe to remove bloom. Pack whole.

Gooseberries Select green, hard and unripe fruit. Top and tail, then cut off a small slice at each end if preserving in syrup to prevent skins from shrivelling. Use a stainless steel knife to cut the fruit.

Loganberries Select firm, deep red fruit. Remove stalks and discard any fruit which has been attacked by maggots.

Mulberries Bottle freshly picked fruit that is not overripe.

Peaches or Nectarines A free-stone variety is best so that the stone may be removed easily. Pour freshly boiling water over fruit, or plunge the fruit into a pan of boiling water, and leave for 30–60 seconds. Drain and skin. Halve the peaches and remove their stones. Work quickly as peaches discolour on standing.

Pears (cooking) Firm cooking pears should be prepared as for dessert pears, then poached in medium syrup until tender. Use the cooking syrup for packing the fruit.

Pears (dessert) Select fruit that is just ripe, for example Conference or William's. Peel, halve and scoop out cores with any loose fibrous flesh. Submerge prepared fruit in acidulated water (water with lemon juice added) or lemon juice until ready to pack. Drain or rinse before packing if the flavour of the lemon juice is not required.

Plums Select Victoria plums that are fully grown, firm and just turning pink. Select purple varieties that are still bright red. Yellow plums should be firm and lemon-yellow in colour. Trim and wipe to remove bloom. Free-stone varieties may be halved and stoned, others should be left whole.

Raspberries Fruit must not be overripe. Pack freshly picked raspberries.

Rhubarb Select tender young rhubarb. Cut it into short lengths and pack. For a tight pack (not quite a solid pack), soak the prepared rhubarb in medium syrup for 8–12 hours. The rhubarb shrinks during soaking. When hard water is used for bottling rhubarb, a harmless white deposit collects on the liquid, so use boiled or softened water to avoid this.

Strawberries Hull the fruit. Soak prepared strawberries in syrup as for rhubarb.

Processing Methods

Follow these instructions very closely. When packing different fruits together, follow the highest temperature and longest processing time suggested for the types of fruit used.

Quick Deep Pan Method

1 Prepare the syrup or bottling liquid and the fruit. Pack the fruit into prepared jars and heat the syrup or bottling liquid to 60°C/140°F.

2 Have ready a saucepan deep enough to submerge the jars. Place a rack, wooden slats or a thick pad of newspaper in the bottom of the pan, then half fill it with water. Heat the water to 38°C/100°F.

3 Check the temperature of the syrup or packing liquid, making sure it is still 60°C/140°F, then pour it into the jars. Dislodge any air bubbles from between the pieces of fruit by gently shaking the jars. The jars should be just overflowing with liquid.

4 Dip rubber rings (if used) in boiling water and put them on the jars. Fix the lids with metal clips. Put on screw bands, tighten them, then undo them by a quarter turn to allow room for each jar to expand as it is heated.

5 Stand the jars in the saucepan and make sure that they are submerged in the water. The jars must not touch each other or the side of the pan.

6 Cover the pan and bring the water to 90°C/194°F in 20–25 minutes. Simmer for time indicated in chart below. Using wooden tongs, transfer jars to a wooden surface. Tighten screw bands, if used. Clips should hold properly without attention. Leave for 24 hours.

7 Test the seal on each jar by removing the screw bands or clips and lifting the jars by their lids. If the lids stay firm they are properly sealed. Label and store.

Processing times for Quick Deep Pan Method

The following times are for jars with a maximum capacity of 1 litre/1¾ pints:

2 minutes	apple rings, blackberries, currants, gooseberries (for cooked puddings), loganberries, mulberries, raspberries, rhubarb (for cooked puddings), damsons and strawberries
10 minutes	apricots, cherries, gooseberries (for cold desserts), whole plums, greengages, rhubarb (for cold desserts) and solid packs of soft fruit (excluding strawberries)
20 minutes	solid pack apples, nectarines, peaches, pineapples, halved plums and solid pack strawberries
40 minutes	whole tomatoes, pears
50 minutes	tomatoes (in own juice)

Moderate Oven Method

The traditional oven method processes the fruit in the oven before adding the syrup; however, the fruit tends to shrink when processed without the syrup. The following method heats the fruit in the syrup to keep shrinkage to the minimum.

1 Set the oven at 150°C/300°F/gas 2. Fill warmed jars with the prepared fruit.

2 Pour in boiling syrup or the chosen liquids to within 2 cm/¾ inch of the top of each jar.

3 Dip rubber rings (if used) and lids in boiling water and fit them on the jars. Do not fit clips and screw bands.

4 Line a roasting tin with three or four layers of newspaper. Stand the jars 5 cm/2 inches apart on the paper.

5 Put the jars in the middle of the oven and process for the times given in the table opposite.

6 Prepare a clean, dry wooden surface on which to stand the jars. Immediately check that the necks of the jars are clean, wiping them with absorbent kitchen paper, and fit the screw bands or clips. **Do not wipe the jars with a damp cloth or they will crack.**

7 Leave for 24 hours before testing the seal by removing the screw bands or clips and lifting the jars by their lids. If the lids stay firm they are properly sealed. Label and store.

Processing times for Moderate Oven Method

Note 4 (350 ml/12 fl oz) jars require the same processing time as 2 (700 ml/1 pint 3½ fl oz) jars.

30–40 minutes (up to 2 kg/ 4½ lb) or 50–60 minutes (2–4.5 kg/ 4½–10 lb) — apple rings, blackberries, currants, gooseberries (for cooked puddings), loganberries, mulberries, raspberries and rhubarb

40–50 minutes (up to 2 kg/ 4½ lb) or 55–70 minutes (2–4.5 kg/ 4½–10 lb) — apricots, cherries, damsons, gooseberries (for cold desserts), whole plums and rhubarb (for cold desserts)

50–60 minutes (up to 2 kg/ 4½ lb) or 65–80 minutes (2–4.5 kg/ 4½–10 lb) — solid pack apples, nectarines, peaches, pineapple and halved plums

60–70 minutes (up to 2 kg/ 4½ lb) or 75–90 minutes (2–4.5 kg/ 4½–10 lb) — pears

Storing Bottled Fruit

Store the sealed jars or bottles in a cool, dark, dry cupboard.

CLEMENTINES IN VODKA
Illustrated on page 62

1 kg/2¼ lb clementines
100 g/4 oz caster sugar
600 ml/1 pint water
½ vanilla pod
30 ml/2 tablespoons orange flower water
300 ml/½ pint vodka

Remove the leaves, stalks and flower-ends from the clementines. Prick them all over with a darning needle – this helps the syrup to penetrate the skins.

Put the sugar, water and vanilla pod in a saucepan over a low heat, and stir occasionally. When the sugar has dissolved, add the clementines, increase the heat, bring to the boil and simmer, uncovered, for about 25 minutes, until the fruit is tender. Remove the vanilla pod.

Drain the fruit, reserving the syrup. Pack the fruit into two warm, sterilised jars. Divide the orange flower water and vodka between them, then fill up the jars with the syrup. Seal the jars and reverse them gently to blend the liquids.

APRICOTS IN BRANDY

1.8 kg/4 lb apricots
225 g/8 oz sugar
250 ml/8 fl oz brandy

You will need three (450 g/1 lb) preserving jars. Sterilize the jars (see page 75) and drain thoroughly, then warm in an oven set at 120°C/250°F/gas ½. Wash and drain the apricots and prick them with a darning needle. Put 300 ml/½ pint water into a large wide heavy-bottomed saucepan or preserving pan. Add 100 g/4 oz of the sugar; heat gently, stirring, until dissolved.

Add enough of the apricots to cover the base of the pan in a single layer. Bring the syrup back to the boil and remove the riper fruit at once. Firmer fruit should be boiled for 2 minutes, but do not let it become too soft. As the fruit is ready, transfer it to the warmed jars, using a slotted spoon.

Add the remaining sugar to the syrup in the pan, lower the temperature and stir until the sugar has dissolved. Boil the syrup, without stirring, until it registers 105°C/220°F on a sugar thermometer, the thread stage (see page 86). Remove the syrup from the heat.

Measure out 250 ml/8 fl oz of the syrup. Stir in the brandy, then pour the mixture over the apricots, covering them completely.

Process the jars following the instructions and timings given for apricots, either by the Quick Deep Pan Method or by the Moderate Oven Method. When cold, test the seals, label the jars and store for at least 1 month in a cool place before opening.

MAKES ABOUT 1.4 KG/3 LB

FRUIT SYRUPS

Fruit syrups may be made from overripe fruit which is not worth freezing or bottling. The juice is extracted from the fruit, then it is sweetened and processed so that it may be stored until required. Steam juice extractors may be purchased to ease the hot method and for processing large quantities of fruit, including apples.

Extracting the Juice
Cold Method This method yields the best-flavoured juice. Place the fruit in a large china or earthenware bowl and crush it with a wooden spoon. Cover the bowl and leave the fruit for 4–5 days, crushing it daily. During this standing time, the pectin which is naturally present in the fruit breaks down and the juice is released. The process may be speeded up, or tough fruits such as blackcurrants may be encouraged to soften, by adding a pectin-decomposing enzyme purchased from a wine-making supplier.
Hot Method Place the fruit in a bowl over simmering water. Crush the fruit. Add 600 ml/1 pint water for each 1 kg/2¼ lb blackcurrants or 100 ml/3½ fl oz for each 1 kg/2¼ lb blackberries. Other soft fruits do not need water. Heat the fruit gently until the juice flows easily, which will take about 1 hour for 3 kg/6½ lb fruit. Check that the water in the saucepan does not boil dry.
Straining the Juice Strain the juice through a scalded jelly bag into a large bowl. For a clear result strain the juice twice. Achieving a clear result is not essential when making syrups, so the juice may be strained through a sieve lined with scalded muslin.

Sweetening and Processing the Juice
Measure the juice, pour it into a bowl and stir in 600 g/1 lb 5 oz sugar for each 1 litre/1¾ pints. Stir until the sugar dissolves – you may have to stand the bowl over a pan of simmering water.

Have ready thoroughly cleaned strong bottles with screw tops. Boil the tops for 5 minutes. Pour the syrup into the bottles, leaving 2 cm/¾ inch headspace at the top of each. Tighten the caps, then loosen them by a quarter turn. Stand all the bottles on a thick pad of newspaper in a deep saucepan and pour in cold water to come up to the top of the bottles. Wedge pieces of cardboard or crumpled foil between the bottles to hold them upright.

Heat the water to 77°C/170°F and keep it at that temperature for 30 minutes. If the water is brought to 88°C/190°F it must be maintained at this temperature for 20 minutes.

Have ready a clean, dry wooden board. Transfer the bottles to it and tighten their caps at once. Allow to cool, label and store in a cool, dark, dry cupboard.

FREEZER TIP

Instead of bottling the syrup, pour it into suitable freezer containers and freeze when cold. Freezing is the easiest, and safest, storage method.

Savoury Pickles and Preserves

Exchanging pots of chutneys and pickles is a tradition in country towns and villages where every house has a sizeable vegetable plot or a few fruit trees. These versatile preserves are an exciting gift for those who do not have a free annual harvest from which to prepare their own chutneys and pickles, or for anyone who does not have the time to cook but appreciates the results of other people's hard work in the kitchen.

PICKLED HORSERADISH

Fresh horseradish is best for cooking, but it can be hard to come by and available only in the autumn. It can be useful to keep a few jars of pickled horseradish in the larder.

horseradish roots

vinegar

salt

Wash the roots in hot water, peel off the skin, then either grate or mince them. Pack loosely in small clean jars.

Horseradish does not need to be soaked in brine, but 5 ml/1 tsp salt should be added to each 250 ml/8 fl oz vinegar used for filling the jars. Pour the salted vinegar over the horseradish to cover, close the jars tightly with vinegar-proof lids and store in a cool, dark place.

MRS BEETON'S TIP

Leave the seeds in the chillies if you like a fiery chutney. For a milder result, remove them. Always take great care when working with chillies not to touch your lips or eyes; a strong reaction may occur on delicate skin. Wash your hands very carefully after chopping the chillies.

PICCALILLI

Illustrated on page 62

This colourful pickle is made from mixed vegetables. In addition to the selection below, chopped peppers (green, yellow and red), tender young broad beans, shallots or marrow may be used. The prepared mixed vegetables should weigh about 1 kg/2¼ lb.

450 g/1 lb green tomatoes, diced

½ small firm cauliflower, broken into florets

1 small cucumber, peeled, seeded and cubed

2 onions, roughly chopped

100 g/4 oz firm white cabbage, shredded

50 g/2 oz cooking salt

750 ml/1¼ pints vinegar

12 chillies

225 g/8 oz sugar

25 g/1 oz mustard powder

15 g/½ oz turmeric

30 ml/2 tbsp cornflour

Combine all the vegetables in a large bowl, sprinkle with the salt, cover and leave to stand for 24 hours. Rinse thoroughly, then drain well.

Heat the vinegar in a saucepan with the chillies. Boil for 2 minutes, leave to stand for 30 minutes, then strain the vinegar into a jug and allow to cool.

Combine the sugar, mustard, tumeric and cornflour in a large bowl. Mix to a paste with a little of the cooled vinegar. Bring the rest of the vinegar back to the boil in a saucepan, pour over the blended mixture, return to the pan; boil for 3 minutes.

Remove from the heat, stir in the drained vegetables, pack into clean jars and seal at once with vinegar-proof covers.

MAKES ABOUT 1 KG/2¼ LB

PICKLED PEARS

10 ml/2 tsp whole cloves
10 ml/2 tsp allspice berries
5 ml/1 tsp crushed cinnamon stick
small piece of root ginger, bruised
225 g/8 oz sugar
300 ml/½ pint vinegar
1 kg/2¼ lb cooking pears

Crush the spices together and tie in a piece of muslin. Combine the sugar and vinegar in a saucepan. Add the muslin bag and heat until the sugar has dissolved.

Peel and core the pears, cut into eighths and simmer gently in the sweetened spiced vinegar until tender but not overcooked or broken. Lift out and pack in warm clean jars. Remove the muslin bag, pressing it to extract the liquid.

Continue to boil the vinegar until it thickens slightly, then pour it over the pears to fill each jar. Leave until cold, then seal securely with vinegar-proof covers. Label and store in a cool, dry place for 2–3 months before use.

MAKES ABOUT 1.25 KG/2¾ LB

PICKLED NASTURTIUM SEEDS

Pickled nasturtium seeds are a good substitute for capers.

nasturtium seeds
brine in the proportion 100 g/4 oz salt to 1 litre/
1¾ pints water
Spiced Vinegar (page 32)
tarragon leaves (optional)

Gather the seeds while still green on a dry day. Steep them in a bowl of brine for 24 hours.

Set the oven at 150°C/300°F/gas 2. Drain the nasturtium seeds, rinse and drain again. Pack in small clean jars so that the contents can be used at once when the jars are opened, place on a baking sheet and warm in the oven for 10 minutes.

Meanwhile boil enough spiced vinegar to cover the seeds. Fill the jars with vinegar, adding a few leaves of tarragon to each, if liked. Store in the refrigerator.

SPICED PEACH PICKLE

2 kg/4½ lb peaches, peeled (see Mrs Beeton's Tip for
Peach Jam, page 68)
20 g/¾ oz whole cloves
20 g/¾ oz allspice berries
1 cinnamon stick, broken in short lengths
1 kg/2¼ lb sugar
1 litre/1¾ pints distilled vinegar

Cut the peaches in half. Remove the stones, crack a few of them and put the kernels in a small saucepan. Add water to cover, bring to the boil over moderate heat and blanch for 3 minutes. Drain.

Tie the spices in muslin and place with the sugar and vinegar in a preserving pan or heavy-bottomed saucepan. Heat gently to dissolve the sugar, then bring to the boil. Lower the heat, stir in the peaches, and simmer until the fruit is just tender, but not overcooked or broken.

Using a slotted spoon, transfer the peach halves to warm clean jars, adding a few of the blanched kernels to each. Continue to boil the liquid in the pan until it thickens, then remove the bag of spices and pour the liquid into the jars. Put on vinegar-proof covers while hot. When cold, label and store in a cool dark place for at least a week.

MAKES ABOUT 3.25 KG/7 LB

MRS BEETON'S TIP

Cinnamon is the dried bark of an evergreen tree belonging to the laurel family. Its sweet aromatic flavour is much valued in cakes, puddings, beef and lamb dishes, where the ground form is generally used. Stick cinnamon is used in pickling, for making mulled drinks, in stewed fruits and to flavour sugar in the same way as a vanilla pod might be used.

BANANA CHUTNEY

....

30 small bananas
1 small onion, sliced
25–50 g/1–2 oz chillies, chopped (see Mrs Beeton's Tip)
1.5 litres/2¾ pints white vinegar
225 g/8 oz seedless raisins
50 g/2 oz salt
50 g/2 oz ground ginger
450 g/1 lb soft light brown sugar

....

Slice the bananas into a large saucepan. Add the remaining ingredients, bring to the boil and cook over moderate heat for 2 hours, stirring occasionally. When the chutney reaches the desired consistency, pour into warm clean jars and cover with vinegar-proof lids. When cool, wipe the jars, label and store in a cool dry place.

MAKES ABOUT 3 KG/6½ LB

....

APPLE CHUTNEY

Illustrated on page 62

....

3 kg/6½ lb apples
2 litres/3½ pints vinegar
1. 5 kg/3¼ 1b sugar
25 g/1 oz salt
10 ml/2 tsp ground allspice
300–400 g/11–14 oz preserved ginger, chopped
1 kg/2¼ lb sultanas, chopped

....

Peel and core the apples; chop them into small pieces. Combine the vinegar, sugar, salt and allspice in a saucepan or preserving pan. Bring to the boil, add the apples, lower the heat and simmer for 10 minutes.

Add the ginger and sultanas to the pan and simmer the mixture until fairly thick. Pour into warm clean jars and cover with vinegar-proof lids. When cool, wipe the jars, label and store in a cool dry place.

MAKES ABOUT 5 KG/11 LB

....

KIWI FRUIT CHUTNEY

....

12 kiwi fruit, peeled and chopped
2 lemons, peeled and roughly chopped
3 onions, grated
1 large banana
150 g/5 oz sultanas or raisins
100 g/4 oz preserved ginger
10 ml/2 tsp salt
5 ml/1 tsp ground ginger
225 g/8 oz brown sugar
2.5 ml/½ tsp pepper
250–300 ml/8 fl oz–½ pint vinegar

....

Combine the kiwi fruit, lemons and onions in a large saucepan. Slice the banana into the pan and stir in all the remaining ingredients, using just enough vinegar to cover. Bring to simmering point and simmer gently for 1½ hours, then mash with a potato masher. Continue to cook until fairly thick, then pour into warm clean jars and cover with vinegar-proof lids. When cool, wipe the jars, label and store in a cool dry place.

MAKES ABOUT 1 KG/2¼ LB

....

MRS BEETON'S TIP

Although kiwi fruit is now associated with New Zealand, it originated in China and was for many years known as the Chinese gooseberry. An excellent source of vitamin C, the fruit is ready to eat when it is slightly soft to the touch. Firmer kiwi fruit – often cheaper than when fully ripe – can be used for this chutney.

GOOSEBERRY CHUTNEY

450 g/1 lb soft light brown sugar
1.5 litres/2¾ pints vinegar
450 g/1 lb onions, finely chopped
675 g/1½ lb seedless raisins
50 g/2 oz mustard seeds, gently bruised
50 g/2 oz ground allspice
50 g/2 oz salt
2 kg/4½ lb gooseberries, topped and tailed

Put the sugar in a large saucepan or preserving pan with half the vinegar. Heat gently, stirring, until the sugar dissolves, then bring to the boil and boil for a few minutes until syrupy. Add the onions, raisins, spices and salt.

Bring the remaining vinegar to the boil in a second pan, add the gooseberries, lower the heat and simmer until tender. Stir the mixture into the large saucepan or preserving pan, cooking until the mixture thickens to the desired consistency. Pour into warm clean jars and cover with vinegar-proof lids. When cool, wipe the jars, label and store in a cool dry place.

MAKES ABOUT 3 KG/6½ LB

MRS BEETON'S TIP

Allspice is a berry grown in the Caribbean area. Its name derives from the flavour, which suggests a blend of cinnamon, nutmeg and cloves. It is added whole to pickles, chutneys, stews and marinades, while the ground form is used in all foods, especially cakes and sweet puddings.

CRANBERRY RELISH

Cranberry relish is delicious with cold roast turkey. Include this in a Christmas hamper and the recipient will have reason to thank you on Boxing Day.

450 g/1 lb cranberries
450 g/1 lb cooking apples, peeled, cored and chopped
450 g/1 lb onions, chopped
450 g/1 lb sugar
1 cinnamon stick
6 cloves
10 allspice berries, coarsely crushed
6 juniper berries, coarsely crushed
2 blades of mace
pared rind of 1 orange
600 ml/1 pint white vinegar

Combine the cranberries, apples and onions in a large saucepan. Add the sugar. Tie all the spices and orange rind together in a square of scalded muslin and add them to the pan.

Pour in the white vinegar and heat the mixture gently, stirring until the sugar has dissolved. Bring to the boil, then lower the heat and cover the pan. Cook the relish gently for 1 hour, stirring occasionally to prevent it from sticking to the base of the pan.

Remove the spices, then pot and cover the relish. Leave it to mature for at least 2 weeks before using. It keeps well for up to a year.

MAKES ABOUT 1.4 KG/3 LB

– Confectionery –

Hand-made sweets and filled chocolates make highly acceptable presents. This chapter includes detailed instructions for confectionery of all types, some simple, others more difficult, to suit your ability and the time you want to spend on creating a unique edible gift.

Home-made Sweets

With good basic equipment, plenty of time, patience and enthusiasm, skills such as working with sugar or tempering chocolate can readily be mastered.

Equipment

A stainless steel or other high-quality saucepan and sugar thermometer are the first items you need. A marble board and large palette knife are best for working boiled sugar syrup, although a plain white (fairly heavy) enamelled tray may be used instead. Some work surfaces withstand the heat of the boiled sugar: other do not. Marble gives the best results.

Chocolate Work Depending on the type of chocolates you hope to make, you may need moulds and/or a dipping fork (a fine, two-pronged fork). To pipe detail on the set chocolates you will need small greaseproof paper icing bags and a small, plain piping nozzle (from shops that supply cake decorating materials).

Simple Tests for Sugar Boiling

A sugar thermometer takes the guesswork out of sweet-making, but syrup can be boiled without stirring and the temperature gauged approximately by using the following tests:

Thread Stage (105°C/220°F) Test by dipping a spoon in the syrup and them pressing another spoon on to the back of it and pulling away. If a thread forms, the syrup is ready.

Blow Stage (110°C/225°F) Test by dipping the top of a metal skewer in the syrup, draining it over the saucepan and then blowing through the hole. A small bubble should form which floats in the air for a second.

Soft Ball Stage (115°C/235°F) Test by dipping about 2.5 ml/½ tsp of the syrup into a bowl of iced water. You should be able to mould the syrup between your fingers to make a soft ball.

Hard Ball Stage (120°C/250°F) Test as for soft ball, but boil for 2–3 minutes longer. A larger, harder ball should be formed.

Small Crack Stage (140°C/275°F) Test by adding a few drops of the mixture to a bowl of iced water. The mixture should become brittle; a thin piece should snap.

Large Crack Stage (155°C/310°F) Test as for small crack, but boil for 2–3 minutes longer. The syrup will be very brittle and will not stick to the teeth when bitten.

Pulling Sugar

In some sweet recipes the boiled sugar mixture is pulled while still warm and pliable to give it a satiny, shiny look. The technique is similar to that employed when making barley sugar. When the syrup has reached the correct temperature, pour it on to an oiled, heat-resistant surface. Allow it to settle for a few minutes until a skin has formed, then using two oiled palette knives, turn the mixture sides to the centre until it cools enough to handle. Oil your hands as a protective measure, then carefully pull the syrup into a sausage shape, working quickly. Fold in the ends, twist and pull again. Repeat the pulling until the candy has a shiny surface. When it is beginning to harden, shape it into a long rope as thick as is needed, and cut quickly into small pieces with oiled scissors. If all the mixture cannot be pulled at once, keep it soft on an oiled baking sheet in a warm place.

Several colours can be introduced by dividing the hot syrup into different portions before cooling, and introducing a few drops of food colouring to each. Pull these separately, then lay them together for the final pulling and shaping. One portion may be left unpulled and clear and added at the final shaping stage.

MARZIPAN FRUITS AND VEGETABLES

White marzipan or almond paste is best for moulding these fruits and vegetables as it can be tinted with food colouring. Study the real vegetable or fruit, or have it in front of you, to achieve the best result. Use icing sugar to dust your fingers.

Colour one small piece of marzipan yellow and another green as the two basic colours. To do this, knead the food colouring into a piece of the marzipan, making the colour quite strong. Small pieces of these colours can be moulded into the remaining marzipan as required. Most fruits and vegetables are painted for optimum effect; this should be done 24 hours after shaping, when the marzipan has dried slightly.

Use cloves to represent the calyx and stalk on fruit. The fine side of a grater is used to simulate the rough skin of citrus fruits. Mould leaves out of marzipan. The fruit can also be half dipped in chocolate or rolled in caster sugar. The marzipan can be moulded around a hazelnut or raisin.

The finished fruits and vegetables may be used to decorate large or small cakes. They may also be packed in sweet cases as a charming gift.

Fruit

Lemon Roll into a ball and ease out to a soft point at each end. Roll lightly on a fine grater.

Apple Roll into a ball, indent top and use a clove for the stalk. Streak with red food colouring.

Pear Gradually taper a ball into shape and put a clove in the narrow end for a stalk. Press another clove well into the rounded end for a calyx. Streak with green food colouring.

Banana Shape into a curved sausage, tapering either end. Colour the tip brown and streak the middle with brown ripening lines using a brown icing pen or food colouring, lightly applied with a brush.

Orange Use orange-coloured marzipan. Mould into a ball and roll on a fine grater.

Strawberry Shape into a ball, then pinch out one end. Paint with red food colouring and sprinkle with caster sugar at once.

Cherries Shape small balls of red marzipan and add long marzipan stalks. These are the ideal shape in which to conceal a hazelnut or raisin.

Peaches Roll into a ball and indent the top, flattening the paste slightly. Brush with a hint of red food colouring.

Vegetables

Parsnips and Carrots Roll into a long cone shape. Mark ridges with a knife or paint these on using thin wisps of brown food colouring. Use orange marzipan for the carrot.

Baby Turnips Use white marzipan. Start with a ball and slightly flatten the top. Paint the top with streaks of purple food colouring and add marzipan leaves.

Mushrooms Cut out a small circle from pink marzipan, and a large piece of white marzipan. Cup the white over the pink, then mark the pink to represent the underside of a mushroom. Add a small stalk.

Cauliflower Press lots of small balls of white marzipan together to represent the florets. Mould leaves from green marzipan and press them around the florets.

Peas Mould small green balls. Mould a thin, open pod and put the green balls in it.

Cabbages Make as for moulded roses, using green marzipan.

SIMPLE TOFFEE

oil for greasing
400 g/14 oz lump sugar
pinch of cream of tartar

Grease a 15 cm/6 inch square baking tin. Put the sugar into a saucepan, add 125 ml/4 fl oz water and heat gently, stirring until the sugar has dissolved. Bring to the boil, add the cream of tartar and boil, without stirring, until the syrup registers 140°C/275°F on a sugar thermometer, the small crack stage (page 86).

When ready, pour the syrup into the prepared tin, leave to cool, then score the surface deeply with a knife, marking it into squares. When set, break into squares as marked, wrap in waxed paper and store in an airtight tin.

MAKES ABOUT 400 G/14 OZ

VARIATIONS

Nut Toffee Add 75 g/3 oz flaked or chopped blanched almonds, or chopped walnuts with the sugar and water.
Ginger Toffee Add 2.5 ml/½ tsp ground ginger with the water.
Vanilla Toffee Add 2.5 ml/½ tsp vanilla essence with the cream of tartar.

BARLEY SUGAR

oil for greasing
30 ml/2 tbsp pearl barley
450 g/1 lb lump sugar
juice of ½ lemon
pinch of cream of tartar

Put the barley in a saucepan with 300 ml/½ pint cold water. Bring to the boil, drain and rinse the barley under cold water. Return it to the clean pan and add 1 litre/1¾ pints cold water. Bring to the boil, lower the heat and simmer, covered, for about 1¾ hours.

Strain the mixture into a measuring jug. Make up to 500 ml/18 fl oz with cold water. Put the sugar in a heavy-bottomed saucepan with the barley water. Stir over low heat for 3–4 minutes until the sugar has dissolved. Increase the heat and boil, without stirring, until the syrup registers 115°C/235°F on a sugar thermometer, the soft ball stage (page 86).

Add the lemon juice and continue boiling until the syrup reaches 155°C/310°F, the large crack stage (page 86).

Pour the mixture on to a lightly oiled slab or large flat laminated board. Allow to cool for a few minutes, then fold the sides of the centre, using an oiled palette knife. Cut into strips with oiled scissors, and twist each strip. When cold and set, store in an airtight jar.

MAKES ABOUT 375 G/13 OZ

EVERTON TOFFEE

A tin of toffees, each lovingly wrapped in waxed paper or cellophane, is a splendid present.

oil for greasing
200 g/7 oz granulated sugar
75 g/3 oz soft light brown sugar
pinch of cream of tartar
10 ml/2 tsp lemon juice
50 g/2 oz butter

Grease a 20 cm/8 inch square baking tin. Combine the sugars in a saucepan, add 175 ml/6 fl oz water and heat gently, stirring until all the sugar has dissolved. Bring to the boil, add the cream of tartar and boil without stirring until the syrup registers 140°C/275°F on a sugar thermometer, the small crack stage (page 86). Add the lemon juice and butter and continue boiling, without stirring, until the syrup reaches 155°C/310°F, the large crack stage (page 86).

Pour the mixture immediately into the prepared tin. When beginning to set score the surface deeply with a knife, marking it into squares. When set, break into squares as marked, wrap in waxed paper and store in an airtight tin.

MAKES ABOUT 350 G/12 OZ

Friandises (page 98), Marzipan Fruits (page 87) and Rum Truffles (page 99) are easy to make and a treat to recieve.

RUSSIAN TOFFEE

oil for greasing
400 g/14 oz sugar
200 g/7 oz redcurrant jelly
100 g/4 oz butter
125 ml/4 fl oz single cream
pinch of cream of tartar
2.5 ml/½ tsp vanilla essence

Grease a 20 cm/8 inch square baking tin. Combine the sugar, redcurrant jelly, butter and cream in a saucepan. Heat gently, stirring, until all the sugar has dissolved. Add the cream of tartar and bring to the boil, stirring frequently. Boil, without stirring, until the mixture registers 120°C/250°F on a sugar thermometer, the hard ball stage (page 86).

Pour immediately into the prepared tin and score the surface deeply with a knife, marking it into squares. When set, separate into squares as marked, wrap in waxed paper and/or coloured cellophane and pack in an airtight tin, jar or bag.

MAKES ABOUT 675 G/1½ LB

PEANUT BRITTLE

Illustrated on page 93

oil for greasing
300 g/11 oz unsalted peanuts
350 g/12 oz granulated sugar
150 g/5 oz soft light brown sugar
150 g/5 oz golden syrup
50 g/2 oz butter
1.25 ml/¼ tsp bicarbonate of soda

Grease a 20 cm/8 inch square baking tin. Spread out the nuts on a baking sheet and warm them very gently in an oven at 150°C/300°F/gas 2. Meanwhile combine the sugars, golden syrup and 125 ml/4 fl oz water in a heavy-bottomed saucepan and heat gently, stirring, until all the sugar has dissolved.

Add the butter, bring to the boil and boil gently, without stirring, until the syrup registers 155°C/310°F on a sugar thermometer, the large crack stage (page 86). Stir in the bicarbonate of soda and the warmed nuts.

Pour the mixture into the prepared tin. When almost set, score the surface deeply with a knife, marking it into bars. When set, break as marked, wrap in waxed paper and pack in an airtight tin.

MAKES ABOUT 1 KG/2¼ LB

MRS BEETON'S TIP

Use a strong, heavy-bottomed saucepan for sweet-making, to prevent mixture sticking and burning. Syrups and sugar-based mixtures tend to rise very quickly during cooking, so make sure you use a large enough pan.

Fondant Sweets (page 100) and Hand-made Chocolates (page 101) can be beautifully packed to make a very special gift

BUTTERSCOTCH

Illustrated opposite

•••••••••••••••••••••••••••••••••

oil for greasing
100 g/4 oz caster sugar
100 g/4 oz butter
75 ml/3 fl oz liquid glucose
125 ml/4 fl oz single cream

Grease an 18 cm/7 inch square baking tin. Combine all the ingredients in a large heavy-bottomed saucepan. Heat very gently, stirring, until the caster sugar has dissolved. Bring to the boil and boil, without stirring, until the mixture registers 140°C/275°F on a sugar thermometer, the small crack stage (page 86).

Pour the mixture immediately into the prepared tin. When beginning to set, score the surface deeply with a knife, marking it into squares. When set, break into squares as marked, wrap in waxed paper and store in an airtight tin.

MAKES ABOUT 225 G/8 OZ

MRS BEETON'S TIP

For a special gift, overwrap each piece of butterscotch in brightly coloured cellophane paper, twist the ends and pack in a decorative box or tin.

CHOCOLATE CARAMELS

•••••••••••••••••••••••••••••••••

oil for greasing
150 g/5 oz caster sugar
15 ml/1 tbsp drinking chocolate powder
75 ml/5 tbsp milk
15 ml/1 tbsp liquid glucose
100 g/4 oz butter
75 ml/5 tbsp single cream
2.5 ml/½ tsp vanilla essence

Grease an 18 cm/7 inch square baking tin. Combine the sugar, chocolate powder, milk and glucose in a heavy-bottomed saucepan. Add one third of the butter and heat gently, stirring until all the sugar has dissolved.

Bring the mixture rapidly to the boil, stirring to prevent burning, and boil until the mixture registers 110°C/225°F on a sugar thermometer, the blow stage (page 86).

Stir in half the remaining butter and boil for 5 minutes more or until the mixture registers 112°C/230°F. Remove the pan from the heat and quickly stir in the remaining butter, with the cream and vanilla essence.

Return the pan to the heat. Stirring constantly, boil the mixture until it registers 115°C/235°F, the soft ball stage (page 86). Pour into the prepared tin. When beginning to set, score the surface deeply with a knife, marking it into squares. When set, cut into squares as marked.

MAKES ABOUT 300 G/11 OZ

MRS BEETON'S TIP

Grated chocolate may be used instead of the drinking chocolate powder, if preferred. You will need about 75 g/3 oz.

All ready for wrapping – Creamy Fudge (page 95), Peanut Brittle (page 90), Buttered Brazils (page 96), Butterscotch and Mint Humbugs (page 96).

CREAMY FUDGE

Illustrated on page 93

oil for greasing
400 g/14 oz sugar
125 ml/4 fl oz milk
50 g/2 oz butter
2.5 ml/½ tsp vanilla essence

Grease an 18 cm/7 inch square baking tin. Combine all the ingredients except the vanilla essence in a large saucepan. Heat gently until the sugar has dissolved, then bring to the boil.

Boil, stirring constantly, until the mixture registers 115°C/235°F on a sugar thermometer, the soft ball stage (page 86). Remove the pan from the heat and stir in the vanilla essence. Cool for 2 minutes, then beat the mixture until it becomes thick and creamy.

Pour into the prepared tin. When nearly set, score the surface of the fudge deeply with a knife, marking it into squares. When set, cut into squares as marked and store in an airtight tin lined with waxed paper.

MAKES ABOUT 450 G/1 LB

MRS BEETON'S TIP

Fudge crystallizes if the sugar is not dissolved properly and if crystals are allowed to form on the sides of the saucepan. To prevent this happening, either grease the saucepan lightly with a little of the butter used in the recipe or cover the saucepan with a lid as soon as the mixture comes to the boil. The steam will wash down the sides of the pan. Remove the lid after 2–3 minutes and boil without stirring until the soft ball stage is reached. The crystals may also be brushed down from the sides of the pan into the mixture, using a clean brush dipped in cold water.

CHOCOLATE FUDGE

oil for greasing
400 g/14 oz sugar
50 g/2 oz golden syrup
50 g/2 oz butter
25 g/1 oz cocoa
75 ml/5 tbsp milk
45 ml/3 tbsp single cream

Grease a 15 cm/6 inch square cake tin. Combine all the ingredients in a heavy-bottomed saucepan and heat gently until all the sugar has dissolved. Bring to the boil.

Boil, stirring constantly, until the mixture registers 115°C/235°F on a sugar thermometer, the soft ball stage (page 86). Cool for 5 minutes, then beat the fudge until creamy and matt in appearance.

Pour the fudge into the prepared tin. Leave until cold before cutting into squares. Store in an airtight tin lined with waxed paper.

MAKES ABOUT 450 G/1 LB

VARIATION

Chocolate Nut Fudge Add 100 g/4 oz chopped walnuts or almonds during the final beating.

MRS BEETON'S TIP

It is important to observe the short cooling time before beating fudge, but the mixture must not overcool or it will be difficult to pour it into the prepared tin.

Teatime Treats include Coconut Ice and Turkish Delight (both on page 97) and Nougat (page 98).

BUTTERED ALMONDS, WALNUTS OR BRAZILS

Illustrated on page 93

Brown, buttery and practically irresistible, buttered nuts make a most acceptable gift. Set each one in an individual fluted paper case and pack in a pretty box or tin.

oil for greasing
50 g/2 oz blanched almonds, halved walnuts or whole Brazil nuts
200 g/7 oz demerara sugar
10 ml/2 tsp liquid glucose
pinch of cream of tartar
50 g/2 oz butter

Spread out the nuts on an oiled baking sheet and warm them very gently in a 150°C/300°F/gas 2 oven. Put the sugar into a saucepan, add 90 ml/6 tbsp water and heat gently, stirring, until the sugar has dissolved.

Bring the mixture to the boil. Add the glucose, cream of tartar and butter. When the butter has dissolved, boil the mixture until it registers 140°C/275°F on a sugar thermometer, the small crack stage (page 86).

Using a teaspoon, pour a little toffee over each nut; it should set very quickly. When cold, remove all the nuts from the baking sheet, wrap separately in waxed paper, and store in an airtight container. Alternatively, gift wrap as suggested above.

MAKES ABOUT 50 ALMONDS, 20 WALNUTS
OR 15 BRAZILS

MINT HUMBUGS

Illustrated on page 93

oil for greasing
400 g/14 oz sugar
75 ml/5 tbsp liquid glucose
2.5 ml/½ tsp cream of tartar
2.5 ml/½ tsp oil of peppermint or to taste
few drops of green food colouring

Combine the sugar and glucose in a saucepan. Add 250 ml/8 fl oz water and heat gently, stirring until the sugar has dissolved. Add the cream of tartar, bring to the boil and boil until the mixture registers 140°C/275°F on a sugar thermometer, the small crack stage (page 86).

Remove the pan from the heat and add peppermint oil to taste. Pour on to a lightly oiled slab or large plate. Divide in half, adding green colouring to one portion.

Allow the mixture to cool until workable, then pull each portion separately as described on page 86. Using oiled scissors cut into 1 cm/½ inch pieces, turning the rope at each cut. When cold and hard wrap each of the humbugs in waxed paper and store in an airtight tin.

MAKES ABOUT 375 G/13 OZ

FRUIT DROPS

If you like the idea of stocking your pantry with a supply of these sweets, as gifts and donations to bazaars, it may be worthwhile investing in a set of old-fashioned metal sweet rings, if you can find them.

fat for greasing
200 g/7 oz sugar
10 ml/2 tsp liquid glucose
pinch of cream of tartar
flavourings and colourings

If using sweet rings, grease them thoroughly and place on a greased baking sheet. Alternatively, grease a 15 cm/6 inch square baking tin.

Combine the sugar and glucose in a saucepan, add 50 ml/2 fl oz water and heat gently, stirring until the sugar has dissolved. Add the cream of tartar, bring to the boil and boil until the mixture registers 120°C/250°F on a sugar thermometer, the hard ball stage (page 86). Remove from the heat and allow to cool for 5 minutes.

Add the flavouring and colouring. Stir the syrup with a wooden spoon, pressing a little syrup against the sides of the pan to give it a grainy appearance.

Pour the syrup at once into the rings or in a 1 cm/½ inch layer in the prepared baking tin. Mark at once into squares and break into pieces when cold.

MAKES ABOUT 200 G/7 OZ

Flavourings and Colourings
Marry fruit flavourings with appropriate food colourings, such as lemon flavouring with pale yellow or green.

PEPPERMINT CREAMS

These simple sweets require no cooking so, they are the ideal present for youngsters to prepare. The paste can be cut into a variety of shapes – hearts for Valentine's Day or holly leaves for Christmas.

400 g/14 oz icing sugar, plus extra for dusting
2 egg whites
10 ml/2 tsp peppermint essence

Sift the icing sugar into a bowl. Work in the egg white and peppermint essence and mix to a moderately firm paste. Knead well, then roll out on a board lightly dusted with icing sugar to a thickness of about 5 mm/¼ inch. Cut into small rounds.

Arrange the peppermint creams on baking sheets covered with greaseproof paper and leave to dry for 12 hours, turning each sweet once. Store in an airtight container lined with waxed paper.

MAKES ABOUT 48

COCONUT ICE

Illustrated on page 94

oil for greasing
300 g/11 oz sugar
2.5 ml/½ tsp liquid glucose
100 g/4 oz desiccated coconut
few drops of pink food colouring

Thoroughly grease a 15 cm/6 inch square baking tin. Put the sugar into a saucepan, add 125 ml/4 fl oz water and heat gently, stirring until all the sugar has dissolved.

Add the glucose, bring to the boil and boil until the mixture registers 115°C/235°F on a sugar thermometer, the soft ball stage (page 86). Remove the pan from the heat and add the coconut. Stir as little as possible, but shake the pan to mix the syrup and coconut.

Pour the mixture quickly into the prepared tin and leave to set. Do not scrape any mixture left in the pan into the tin, as it will be sugary. Top with a layer of pink coconut ice as suggested in Mrs Beeton's Tip.

MAKES ABOUT 400 G/14 OZ OF EACH COLOUR

TURKISH DELIGHT

Illustrated on page 94

25 g/1 oz gelatine
400 g/14 oz sugar
1.25 ml/¼ tsp citric acid
2.5 ml/½ tsp vanilla essence
10 ml/2 tsp triple-strength rose water
few drops of pink food colouring (optional)
50 g/2 oz icing sugar
25 g/1 oz cornflour

Place 250 ml/8 fl oz water in a large saucepan. Sprinkle the gelatine on to the liquid. Set aside for 15 minutes until the gelatine is spongy. Add the sugar and citric acid, place the saucepan over gentle heat, and stir constantly until dissolved. Bring the mixture to the boil and boil for 20 minutes without stirring. Remove from the heat and allow to stand for 10 minutes.

Stir in the vanilla essence, rose water and colouring if used. Pour into a wetted 15 cm/6 inch square baking tin. Leave uncovered in a cool place for 24 hours.

Sift the icing sugar and cornflour together on to a sheet of greaseproof paper. Turn the Turkish delight on to the paper and cut into small squares, using a sharp knife dipped in the icing sugar mixture. Toss well in the mixture, so that all sides are coated. Pack in airtight containers lined with waxed paper and dusted with the remaining icing sugar and cornflour.

MAKES ABOUT 500 G/18 OZ

MRS BEETON'S TIP

To achieve the traditional pink and white effect, make two separate batches of coconut ice, colouring the second batch pale pink and pouring it on to the set white mixture. It is advisable to make two separate quantities of coconut ice, rather than to add colouring to half the first mixture, as the extra stirring will make the mixture grainy. Add the pink food colouring to the second batch just before it reaches soft ball stage.

NOUGAT
Illustrated on page 94

· ·

50 g/2 oz blanched almonds, chopped
225 g/8 oz icing sugar
5ml/1 tsp liquid glucose
50 g/2 oz honey
1 egg white
25 g/1 oz glacé cherries, chopped

Line the sides and base of a 15 × 10 cm/6 × 4 inch baking tin with rice paper. Spread out the almonds on a baking sheet and brown them lightly under a preheated grill. Watch them carefully; they will soon scorch if left. Whisk the egg white in a heatproof bowl until stiff.

Combine the sugar, glucose, honey and 30 ml/2 tbsp water in a small saucepan. Stir over very low heat until melted; boil until the mixture registers 140°C/275°F on a sugar thermometer, the small crack stage (page 86). This takes only a few minutes. Remove from the heat. Whisking all the time, trickle the syrup into the egg white and continue whisking until the mixture is very glossy and beginning to stiffen.

Stir in the almonds and cherries. Turn the mixture into the prepared tin and press it down well. Cover with a single layer of rice paper. Place a light, even weight on top and leave until quite cold. Cut into oblong pieces or squares and wrap in waxed paper. Store in an airtight container.

MAKES ABOUT 200 G/7 OZ

FRANDISES
Illustrated on page 88

· ·

oil for greasing
8 cherries
8 grapes
8 small strawberries
1 satsuma, in segments
200 g/7 oz granulated sugar
8 Brazil nuts

Prepare the fruit, leaving the stems on the cherries, grapes and strawberries. Remove any pith from the satsuma segments. Generously grease a large baking sheet and have ready two oiled forks.

Put the sugar in a heavy-bottomed saucepan and add 175 ml/6 fl oz water. Heat gently, stirring until the sugar has dissolved. Increase the heat and boil the syrup until it turns a pale gold in colour. Immediately remove the pan from the heat and dip the bottom of the pan in cold water to prevent the syrup from darkening any further.

Spear a fruit or nut on a fork, dip it in the hot caramel syrup, then allow the excess caramel to drip back into the pan. Use the second fork to ease the fruit or nut on to the baking sheet. Continue until all the fruits and nuts have been glazed, warming the syrup gently if it becomes too thick to use.

When the coating on all the fruits and nuts has hardened, lift them carefully off the baking sheet. Serve in paper sweet cases.

MAKES ABOUT 48

RUM TRUFFLES

Illustrated on page 88

50 g/2 oz nibbed almonds
150 g/5 oz plain chocolate, in squares
150 g/5 oz ground almonds
30 ml/2 tbsp double cream
75 g/3 oz caster sugar
15 ml/1 tbsp rum
grated chocolate or chocolate vermicelli for coating

Spread out the almonds on a baking sheet and toast them lightly under a preheated grill. Bring a saucepan of water to the boil.

Put the chocolate in a heatproof bowl that will fit over the pan of water. When the water boils, remove the pan from the heat, set the bowl over the water and leave until the chocolate has melted.

Remove the bowl from the pan and stir in the toasted almonds, ground almonds, cream, sugar and rum. Mix to a stiff paste.

Roll the paste into small balls and toss at once in grated chocolate or chocolate vermicelli. Serve in sweet paper cases.

MAKES ABOUT 15

GANACHE TRUFFLES

Ganache is a rich chocolate cream, made by melting chocolate with cream, then allowing it to set. The chocolate cream may be whipped before it is firm to make a rich topping for cakes; for truffles the mixture is chilled until it is firm enough to be shaped and coated.

350 g/12 oz plain chocolate
300 ml/½ pint double cream
5 ml/1 tsp vanilla essence
15 ml/1 tbsp icing sugar cocoa for coating

Break the chocolate into squares and place them in a small saucepan. Add the cream and heat gently, stirring often, until the chocolate melts. Remove from the heat and stir in the vanilla, then allow to cool, stirring the mixture occasionally.

Chill the mixture until it is firm enough to shape. Place the cocoa in a small basin. Use two teaspoons to shape small balls of mixture and drop them in the cocoa one at a time. Turn the truffles in the cocoa to coat them completely, then place them on a plate or baking sheet and chill again until firm.

MAKES ABOUT 25

MRS BEETON'S TIP

Ganache can be piped quite successfully: leave the mixture to cool, then chill it lightly until thickened but not set. Whip the mixture until it is lighter in colour and of a piping consistency. Spoon the whipped ganache into a piping bag fitted with a star nozzle and pipe it into paper sweet cases. Chill until set, then dust with icing sugar.

Fondant Sweets

Traditional fondant (not to be confused with moulding icing or sugar paste) is widely used by commercial confectioners as an icing for petits fours as it sets to a dry, shiny finish that remains soft inside. It is also used as a filling for chocolates. Some specialist cake decorating suppliers and shops sell fondant icing mix in a powdered form. This is a boon because small quantities can be made following the packet instructions. You will need a sugar thermometer to make traditional boiled fondant. A fondant mat is a very useful piece of equipment for sweet making. It consists of a sheet of plastic about 2 cm/¾ inch deep, with fancy shapes inset, into which the liquid fondant, jelly or chocolate is poured. When set, sweets can be removed by bending back the sheet.

450 g/1 lb caster or lump sugar
20 ml/4 tsp liquid glucose
stock syrup (see Mrs Beeton's Tip)

Put the sugar in a heavy-bottomed saucepan which is absolutely free from grease. Add 150 ml/ ¼ pint water and heat gently until the sugar has completely dissolved. Stir very occasionally and use a wet pastry brush to wipe away any crystals that form on the sides of the pan. When the sugar has dissolved add the liquid glucose and boil to 115°C/240°F, the soft ball stage (page 86), without stirring. Keep the sides of the pan clean by brushing with the wet brush when necessary. Remove from the heat and allow the bubbles in the mixture to subside. Pour the mixture slowly into the middle of a wetted marble slab and allow to cool a little. Work the sides to the middle with a sugar scraper or palette knife to make a smaller mass.

With a wooden spoon in one hand and a scraper in the other, make a figure of eight with the spatula, keeping the mixture together with the scraper. Work until the whole mass is completely white. Break off small amounts and knead well, then knead together to form a ball.

If not using it immediately, store the fondant in a screw-topped jar or wrap it closely in cling film and place it in a sealed polythene bag in an airtight container.

Peppermint Softies Dust a fondant mat with cornflour. Soften 300 ml/11 oz fondant in a bowl over hot water. Do not overheat it. Add a few drops of peppermint essence and enough stock syrup to make a cream with the consistency of thick pouring cream. Pour into the prepared mat and set overnight. Makes about 300 g/11 oz.

Walnut Fondant Colour 100 g/4 oz fondant pale green and flavour with pineapple essence. Set out 36 walnut halves. Divide the fondant into 18 equal portions and roll them into balls. Flatten into pieces about the same diameter as the walnuts. Sandwich one piece of the fondant between two walnut halves, pressing firmly. Allow the sweets to harden in a dry, warm place. Serve in paper sweet cases.

Fondant Fruits or Nuts Any firm fruit that will not discolour may be used. Clean and dry the fruit, removing any stones or pips. Divide oranges or mandarins into segments. To coat 18–20 small fruits or 36–40 nuts, you will need about 200 g/7 oz fondant. Warm the fondant in a bowl over hot water, stirring it until it has the appearance of thick cream. Add some stock syrup if necessary. Dip the fruits or nuts individually in the fondant and place on a plate to dry. Cherries and grapes can be held by the stem, but other fruits and nuts must be immersed and lifted out with a fork. Use within two days.

MRS BEETON'S TIP

To make about 200 ml/7 fl oz stock syrup, heat 150 g/5 oz sugar with 150 ml/¼ pint water in a saucepan. Stir occasionally until the sugar has dissolved, then boil without stirring for 3 minutes. Use a spoon to remove any scum that rises to the surface. Cool, then strain into a screw-topped jar and close tightly. The syrup may be stored in a cool place (not the refrigerator) for up to 2 months.

Hand-made Chocolates

Many of the sweets in this chapter are suitable for coating with chocolate, but the process takes time and patience. Couverture chocolate should ideally be used, but must be tempered first (see below).

Alternatively, use a super-fatted commercial dipping or coating chocolate. The flavour may not be quite so good as that of couverture, but the product is much easier to use: simply break it into small pieces and melt in a bowl over a saucepan of hot water.

Tempering Couverture Chocolate Break the chocolate into pieces and put it in a bowl over a saucepan of hot water. Stirring frequently, heat to about 50°C/120°F, then allow the chocolate to cool again until it thickens (at about 28°C/82°F). Heat again to about 31°C/88°F; thin enough to use but thick enough to set quickly.

DIPPING FOOD IN CHOCOLATE

Biscuits, choux buns, nuts, marzipan shapes, real leaves and fruits such as maraschino cherries, grapes, raisins, dates and slices of banana can all be dipped in melted chocolate. They can be part-dipped or fully dipped according to the effect required. Special dipping forks have two long prongs that are bent at the ends to stop the food falling off when dipped. Alternatively, use a corn-on-the-cob fork, cocktail stick or two fine skewers, one on either side of the food. For larger pieces of food such as choux buns, or hard foods such as almonds, it is best to use your fingers to dip the ingredients.

Melt the chocolate by breaking it into squares and placing it in a heatproof bowl. Stand the bowl over a pan of hot water and stir the chocolate until it has melted. Do not allow the water to simmer rapidly or boil as it will overheat the chocolate. Do not allow any water or condensation to enter the chocolate or it will separate and curdle. For dipping food the consistency should be thick enough to coat the back of a spoon.

If the chocolate is too thin, remove the bowl from the pan and leave it to cool slightly, until the chocolate thickens. Keep the chocolate warm (over the saucepan of water), while you are working. If the chocolate becomes too thick, remove the bowl, reheat the water, then replace the bowl. Stir the chocolate occasionally as you are dipping the food.

You will need a good depth of melted chocolate to dip food successfully; it should be at least 5 cm/ 2 inches deep. (When the chocolate becomes too shallow for successful dipping, do not discard it; stir the excess into buttercreams or similar icings to avoid wastage.)

Line a baking sheet or wire rack with a sheet of waxed paper or non-stick baking parchment. Have ready all the food to be dipped and start with firm items, such as nuts and marzipan. Finish with soft foods, such as fruits. Plunge the food into the chocolate to the depth required, then quickly withdraw it at the same angle at which it was plunged. Do not rotate part-dipped food in the chocolate or the top line of chocolate will be uneven. Gently shake the food to allow the excess chocolate to fall back into the bowl, then place it on the prepared sheet or rack to dry.

Centres for Coating in Chocolate

Marzipan Colour and flavour marzipan, cut into attractive shapes and dip in melted chocolate.

Fondant Colour, flavour, cut into shapes and allow to dry, then dip in melted chocolate.

Ginger or Pineapple Cut preserved ginger or glacé pineapple into small pieces, then dip in melted chocolate.

Nuts Dip blanched almonds, Brazil nuts or walnuts in melted chocolate.

Caramels, Toffee or Nougat Cut into squares or rectangles; dip in melted chocolate.

Coconut Ice Dip completely in melted chocolate or just half dip each piece.

CHOCOLATE EGGS

Making chocolate eggs for Easter is fun and very rewarding when you have time to add attractive decorations and finishing touches. There are several different types of moulds, including flexible plastic moulds which allow for easy release of the set chocolate eggs, rigid plastic moulds with a rim which is flexed to release the chocolate and metal moulds which give a very shiny finish to the chocolate but from which it is more difficult to release the egg. The moulds come in various sizes. Each one makes half an egg and matching halves are only joined together when the set chocolate has been unmoulded.

Buy good-quality chocolate that has a good flavour and a firm set. Chocolate-flavoured cake coverings are not suitable. Wash, dry and thoroughly polish the inside of rigid plastic or metal Easter egg moulds with a clean tea-towel. Break the chocolate into a heatproof basin and stand this over a saucepan of hot, not boiling, water. Stir occasionally until the chocolate melts, then remove the basin from the pan. Take care not to allow any water to drip into the chocolate as this will cause it to separate.

Brush a coating of melted chocolate inside the mould and place it in a cool place until just set. Add another coating of chocolate, making it as thick as possible but keeping it even in depth.

Leave the chocolate until it is just set, then continue building up the layers. Stand the basin over a pan of hot water to melt the chocolate again as necessary. The first and second coats of chocolate will usually set in the refrigerator in just a few minutes but once you start to build up the thickness, do not place the chocolate in the refrigerator; instead leave it in a cool room to set. The extreme cold of the refrigerator tends to cause condensation which, if the egg is dried or stored for a long time, may result in the surface becoming dull and whitened.

The chocolate must be allowed to set thoroughly for several hours before the egg can be released. It is a good idea to cover a small board with wax paper and release the egg on to this. The wax paper can be used to slide the egg off the board and to help when turning it over. Cotton gloves are worn by professional confectioners. It is worth buying them from a cake decorating or catering supplier if you intend taking chocolate work seriously. Alternatively, just make sure that your hands are very cool, rinsing them under cold water and drying them thoroughly if necessary, then cover the surface of your hand with a sheet of absorbent kitchen paper and invert the egg on to it from the wax paper. Place the paper and egg on the board rather than cradling it in your hand.

When both egg halves have been released and inverted on the board, support one half with crumpled absorbent kitchen paper or foil. Then brush or pipe some melted chocolate around the rim and carefully invert the second half on top. When the chocolate has set to seal the halves together, the join can be decorated with piped chocolate or with piped royal icing.

Alternatively, apply an occasional spot of chocolate and stick a band of ribbon around the join. Trim the ribbon to length before sticking it on the egg. When the band of ribbon has set in place turn the egg upright and support it in a tissue-lined box. Neaten the top of the egg by sticking a bow of ribbon over the ends of the ribbon band or attach crystallized violets.

Decorative Finishes for Chocolate Eggs

* To pipe chocolate, leave the melted chocolate to cool until it has thickened very slightly, then spoon some into a small greaseproof paper piping bag. Fold the top of the bag over, then snip off the tip of the bag when you are ready to pipe the chocolate. White chocolate can be piped on a dark egg in decorative designs, such as flowers or geometric patterns.

* The mixture for Ganache Truffles (page 99) can be piped around the join in the egg. Fit a small star piping nozzle in a greaseproof paper piping bag and spoon the whipped mixture into it. Rinse your hands under cold water and dry them before piping the mixture as it will melt if your hands are warm.

* Sugar cake decorations are ideal for decorating the side and/or top of an egg. Crystallised violets, angelica, sugar mimosa balls, piped icing flowers and chocolate shapes are all useful. Attach them with a spot of melted chocolate.

* Sweets and chocolates can also be attached to the outside of the egg for decoration. For example, tiny jellied sweets or chocolate drops can be arranged in patterns or flower shapes.

PASTILLAGE EASTER EGGS

Pastillage is a white sugar-based paste used by cake decorators to make models. The paste dries hard and is therefore inedible, but it can be used to make decorative eggs or eggs which can be used as containers for Easter gifts. Pastillage is available as a powder mix from cake decorating suppliers. Follow the packet instructions and knead the paste thoroughly until it is smooth and elastic. Then wrap it in cling film and place it in a closed polythene bag in an airtight container and leave it overnight before using it. Knead well again.

The paste should be moulded over the outside of an Easter egg mould. Dust the mould with cornflour to prevent the paste from sticking and place it upside down on a board. Roll out the paste to about 5 mm/¼ inch thick or slightly less and cover the mould, gently lifting the paste and easing out the creases. Use a fine, sharp knife or scalpel to trim off the excess paste around the bottom. Then tap the edge of the paste neatly all around the mould to give a neat rim on the egg. Leave to dry for several hours or overnight, until the paste is rock hard. Knead any paste trimmings back together, wrap them in cling film and polythene and store them in an airtight container. If the paste is wrapped closely and kept in a cool place, it will remain usable for weeks. The paste will harden slightly and must be kneaded well.

Remove the pastillage egg from the mould when dry. Make a second half to complete the egg. To join the eggs, cover the rim of one half with cling film. Roll out three thin ropes of pastillage and plait them together into a strip long enough to fit around the rim of the second egg half. Stick the plait in place with egg white or by mixing a little of the pastillage to a paste with a few drops of water. The plait should cover the rim of the egg and extend above it slightly. Then carefully place the cling-film covered rim of the second half inside the plait. Ease the edge of the plait out slightly so that there is a narrow gap between it and the cling film, then leave for several hours to dry.

A plain band of paste can be attached instead of a plait, or decorative shapes cut out of rolled-out pastillage can be stuck around the edge. The idea is to make a rim into which the second egg half fits when the paste is dry. The pastillage can be coloured by kneading in concentrated food colouring, then it can be rolled out and cut or shaped into a band or plait for the rim.

When the plait is dry, lift off the egg half with the cling-film-covered rim. Decorate the egg by painting it with food colouring or spraying it gold. When painting, use a concentrated food colour and take care not to make the surface of the paste too wet or it will dissolve slightly. Food or craft decorations can be attached to the egg. Remember that the egg is NOT EDIBLE. Line it with tissue and fill with sweets or a gift.

— Tipples to Share —

This short section includes ideas for alcohol-free drinks as well as true tipples. They make refreshingly different tokens of goodwill and friendship.

LEMONADE

A picnic hamper makes a wonderful summer gift, especially if you include some home-cooked specialities such as a pâté, some savoury biscuits, one or two chutneys or pickles, a teabread and a bottle of home-made lemonade. Add a label with the suggestion that the lemonade be diluted with iced water to serve.

1.8 kg/4 lb sugar
grated rind of 2 lemons
1 litre/1¾ pints lemon juice

Put the sugar in a saucepan with 1 litre/1¼ pints water. Heat gently, stirring until all the sugar has dissolved, then stir in the lemon rind. Boil for 5 minutes without further stirring. Cool. Stir in the lemon juice, strain into clean jugs or bottles and store in the refrigerator.

MAKES ABOUT 3 LITRES/5¼ PINTS

MRS BEETON'S TIP

When making ginger beer, use proper beer bottles as mineral bottles may not be strong enough to withstand the pressures. Wash them thoroughly inside and out, then sterilize them and the closures in a solution of 2 crushed Campden tablets and 2.5 ml/½ tsp citric acid in 500 ml/17 fl oz water.

GINGER BEER

As anyone who has ever experienced the explosion caused by unwisely stored ginger beer will know, fermentation causes strong pressure to build up inside the bottles, so it is important to use sturdy, properly sterilized beer bottles with clip-on bottle seals or screw tops. Store in a cardboard box in a cool dark place, preferably on a concrete floor, and when parting with a bottle as a gift, make sure that the recipient knows how to store it.

25 g/1 oz fresh root ginger, bruised
thinly pared rind and juice of 2 lemons
450 g/1 lb sugar
7.5 ml/1½ tsp cream of tartar
1 sachet dried beer yeast

Combine the ginger, lemon rind, sugar and cream of tartar in a suitable white brewing bucket with lid. Add 5 litres/8½ pints hot water. Stir gently until the sugar has dissolved, then leave to cool.

Add the lemon juice to the cooled liquid and sprinkle the yeast over the surface. Cover and leave in a warm place for 48 hours, skimming off the yeast head after 24 hours. When the fermentation has finished, skim the surface again before bottling.

Thoroughly wash sufficient beer bottles to hold the ginger beer, and sterilize them in Campden solution (see Mrs Beeton's Tip) or by using another suitable wine-making product. Siphon the ginger beer into the bottles, being careful not to disturb the deposit in the bottom of the container. Seal the bottles tightly and leave in a warm place for 3 days. Use at once or store in a cool dark place until required, checking the bottles frequently.

MAKES ABOUT 5 LITRES/8¾ PINTS

Tipples to Share do not have to be alcoholic - Orange Squash and Elderflower Cordial (page 106) and Ginger Beer are as interesting as Sangria (page 107) and Cherry Brandy (page 108). Jars of cloves and bundles of cinnamon are also fun for culinary use or to flavour mulled wine.

ELDERFLOWER CORDIAL

Illustrated on page 105

Diluted with iced water, this makes a refreshing drink.

900 g/2 lb caster sugar
30 g/1¼ oz citric acid • 1 lemon
10 elderflower heads, washed and drained

Put the sugar in a large heatproof bowl. Add 600 ml/ 1 pint boiling water and stir until all the sugar has dissolved. Stir in the citric acid. Grate the lemon and add the rind to the bowl, then slice the fruit. Add the lemon slices to the bowl with the elderflower heads. Cover and allow to stand for 12 hours or overnight. Strain through muslin, bottle and store for 1 month before serving.

MAKES ABOUT 600 ML/1 PINT

ORANGE SQUASH

Illustrated on page 105

Campden tablets, available from wine-making suppliers, consist of sodium metabisulphite. They are used for killing off wild yeasts in fruit when making wine. Adding a Campden tablet to this squash prevents the orange juice from fermenting.

grated rind of 3 oranges • 450 g/1 lb sugar
¼ lemon, cut in wedges
300 ml/½ pint fresh orange juice
1 Campden tablet

Combine the orange rind, sugar and lemon wedges in a saucepan. Add 450 ml/¾ pint water and heat gently, stirring to dissolve the sugar, until boiling. Leave over low heat for 30 minutes, then set aside until cold.

Add the orange juice, stir and strain into a clean jug. Squeeze, then discard the lemon wedges in the strainer. Crush the Campden tablet in a mug and add a little boiling water. Stir until dissolved, then add to the squash. Stir well before pouring into a bottle. Cover and store in the refrigerator for up to 3 weeks. To serve, dilute to taste with water, soda water or mineral water.

MAKES ABOUT 1 LITRE/1¾ PINTS

BARLEY WATER

25 g/1 oz pearl barley
grated rind of 1 lemon
125 ml/4 fl oz lemon juice
sugar to taste

Put the pearl barley in a saucepan with water to cover. Bring to the boil and boil for 2 minutes, then strain into a clean pan. Stir in the lemon rind, juice and 1.1 litres/ 2 pints water. Heat gently, stirring occasionally, until boiling. Reduce the heat, cover the pan and cook gently for 45 minutes. Leave, covered, until cold.

Strain, sweeten to taste, then store in a covered container in the refrigerator for up to 1 week. Alternatively, freeze in ice-cube trays or small containers.

MAKES ABOUT 1.2 LITRES/2¼ PINTS

WELSH NECTAR

With a flavour reminiscent of grape juice, Welsh Nectar is a pleasant alcohol-free drink which can be diluted with soda water or carbonated spring water.

2 lemons• 225 g/8 oz sugar lumps, crushed
225 g/8 oz seedless raisins, minced or finely chopped

Pare the lemons thinly, taking care to avoid the pith. Put the peel in a large heatproof bowl. Add the sugar. Pour over 2.25 litres/4 pints boiling water. Stir until all the sugar has dissolved. Cover and leave to stand until cool.

Squeeze the lemons; strain the juice into the bowl. Stir in the raisins. Pour into a large jar, close tightly and set aside for 4–5 days, stirring several times a day.

Strain the mixture through a jelly bag into clean bottles. Cover and refrigerate. Use within 2 weeks.

MAKES ABOUT 2 LITRES/3½ PINTS

MRS BEETON'S TIP

A coffee filter (cone and paper) can be used to strain the nectar.

SLOE GIN

450 g/1 lb ripe sloes
225 g/8 oz caster sugar
1 litres/1¾ pints dry gin

Remove stalks and leaves from the sloes, then wash and prick them all over. Put them in a jar which can be fitted with an airtight seal.

In a large jug or bowl, dissolve the sugar in the gin and pour it on to the sloes. Cover the jar and store it in a cool dark place for 3 months, giving it a gentle shake ever few days to extract and distribute the fruit flavour. Strain, bottle and store for 3 months more before serving the sloe gin. It is not diluted.

MAKES ABOUT 1.25 LITRES/2¼ PINTS

SANGRIA

Illustrated on page 105

Make this a fun gift for hot summer days. Pour the basic sangria 'mix' into an empty mineral water bottle. Make a fun fruit label by cutting out a wedge of card (or several) and colouring it to look like a segment of orange or lemon. Better still, cut out a picture of a piece of fruit from a magazine and stick it on plain paper. Suggest serving slices of fresh fruit and ice in the sangria mix. Tie the label around the neck of the bottle.

50 g/2 oz sugar
pared rind of 2 oranges
pared rind of 2 limes or lemons
1 bottle of red wine (about 750 ml/1¼ pints)

Put the sugar in a small saucepan with 50 ml/2 fl oz water. Stir over gentle heat until the sugar has dissolved.

Cut the citrus rind into long, narrow strips and place in a large heatproof bowl, pour over the hot syrup and set aside until cool.

Push the citrus rind into a clean bottle, then pour in the syrup and add the wine. Shake lightly.

SERVES 8

NEGUS

Mrs Beeton's Negus had more water and was originally a drink served at children's parties. Sherry or sweet white wine were sometimes used instead of port.

100 g/4 oz sugar lumps
1 lemon
600 ml/1 pint port
grated nutmeg

Rub a few of the sugar lumps over the lemon to absorb the oil. Put all the sugar lumps in a large heatproof jug.

Squeeze the lemon and strain the juice into the jug. Pour in the port. Stir the mixture, crushing the sugar lumps. Add 600 ml/1 pint boiling water, with grated nutmeg to taste. Stir well to dissolve all the sugar, cover the jug and set aside to cool slightly before serving.

SERVES 6 TO 8

RUM AND BRANDY TODDY

This recipe yields a magnificent, warming drink! Include instructions for warming the mixture on the label.

225 g/8 oz sugar lumps
2 large lemons
600 ml/1 pint rum
600 ml/1 pint brandy
5 ml/1 tsp grated nutmeg

Rub a few of the sugar lumps over the lemon to absorb the oil. Put them in a heatproof bowl with the remaining sugar lumps. Squeeze the lemons and strain the juice into the bowl, then crush the sugar with a wooden spoon.

Pour 1.1 litres/2 pints boiling water into the bowl, stir well, then add the remaining ingredients. Mix well. Serve at once.

SERVES 8 TO 10

HOME-MADE NOYEAU

Use this nut-flavoured liqueur to flavour puddings and cakes.

150 ml/¼ pint milk
100 g/4 oz whole unblanched almonds
15 ml/1 tbsp liquid honey
225 g/8 oz caster sugar
grated rind of 1 lemon
1 (700 ml/24 fl oz) bottle Irish whiskey
150 ml/¼ pint single cream

Combine the milk, almonds and honey in a saucepan. Bring to the boil, remove from the heat, cover and leave to stand until quite cold.

Strain the milk into a jug. Grind the almonds in a nut mill or food processor, or use a mortar and pestle.

Transfer the ground almonds to a bowl and stir in the sugar. Add the lemon rind and whiskey, then stir in the cold milk and honey mixture. Add the cream. Pour into a large jar, close tightly and store for 10 days, shaking daily. Pour the mixture through a filter paper into a large jug. Fill small bottles, corking them tightly. Store in a cool, dry place.

MAKES ABOUT 900 ML/1½ PINTS

WHISKEY CORDIAL

450 g/1 lb ripe whitecurrants
grated rind of 2 lemons
100 g/4 oz root ginger, grated
1.1 litres/2 pints Irish whiskey
450 g/1 lb sugar lumps, crushed

Strip the currants from the stalks and put them in a large jug. Add the lemon rind, ginger and whiskey. Cover the jug closely and set it aside for 24 hours.

Strain through a fine sieve into a clean jug, stir in the sugar lumps and leave to stand for 12 hours more, stirring occasionally to dissolve the sugar lumps. Pour into clean bottles, cork tightly and store in a cool dry place.

MAKES ABOUT 1.25 LITRES/2¼ PINTS

ORANGE BRANDY

Illustrated on page 26

A bit of forward planning is required for this present, as the brandy is best stored for a year before being opened. For the best flavour, use Seville oranges.

175 g/6 oz sugar lumps
2 oranges
1 (680 ml/23 fl oz) bottle of brandy

Rub a few of the sugar lumps over the oranges to absorb the oil. Put them in a large bowl with the remaining sugar lumps.

Pare the orange peel in thin strips, taking care to avoid the pith, and add to the bowl. Squeeze the oranges and strain the juice into the bowl. Crush the sugar cubes with a spoon. Stir in the brandy. Pour into a large jar, close tightly and set aside for 3 days, stirring several times a day.

When all the sugar has dissolved, strain the mixture into clean bottles, Cork tightly and store in a cool, dry place. The flavour will improve on keeping, and the brandy should ideally be matured for 1 year.

MAKES ABOUT 1 LITRE/1¾ PINTS

CHERRY BRANDY

Illustrated on page 105

Morello cherries are bitter cherries which are used in cooking rather than for eating raw. These red fruit are used when only just ripe, when they contribute an excellent flavour.

450 g/1 lb cherries, preferably morello
75 g/3 oz sugar
brandy

Place the cherries in perfectly clean jars, sprinkling the sugar between the fruit. The jars should be full but not tightly packed. Top up with brandy to completely cover the cherries. Cover with airtight lids and invert each jar several times to dissolve the sugar. Store in a cool, dark place for 2–3 months before using. The cherries and liquor will keep for at least a year.

GINGER WINE

All the rules which apply to home wine-making must be adopted when preparing this recipe: all equipment must be sterilized using a commercial sterilizing agent and air must be excluded from the wine at all stages in the fermentation and clearing process. Use Campden tablets or a suitable product for arresting the fermentation, then add wine finings to clear the wine or filter it until clear. The bottles and corks must also be sterilized. The quantities given here are only a proportion of those in the original recipe which called for nine gallons of water. The original method was far simpler, based on fermenting the wine in a cask for a fortnight, then adding the brandy and corking down the cask by degrees. Then the wine was left for a few weeks before bottling. If you have a cold cellar or outhouse, you may like to experiment with the old-fashioned method; however, the recipe below is likely to give more reliable results.

---

pared rind and juice of 1 lemon
50 g/2 oz fresh root ginger
1.4 kg/3 lb sugar
1 sachet of wine yeast
100 g/4 oz raisins, chopped
Campden tablets
wine finings or filter
300 ml/½ pint brandy

Place the lemon rind in a large saucepan. Cut the ginger in half and hit both pieces with a meat mallet or rolling pin, then add them to the pan with 450 g/1 lb sugar and 1.1 litres/2 pints water. Stir until the sugar has dissolved, then bring to the boil and cook for 5 minutes. Skim off any scum which rises to the surface of the syrup.

Pour the syrup into a sterilized fermentation bucket and add 1.1 litres/2 pints cold water. Stir in the yeast, cover the bucket and leave in a warm place overnight. Next day, stir in another 450 g/1 lb sugar, the strained lemon juice and another 1.1 litres/2 pints water. Divide the raisins equally between two sterilized fermentation jars. Add a piece of ginger and half the lemon rind from the wine to each jar, then stir the liquid well to ensure that all the sugar has dissolved and divide it between the jars. Fit airlocks on the jars and leave them in a warm place.

When the initial fierce fermentation has subsided (about 3 days), place the remaining sugar in a saucepan with 1.1 litres/2 pints water and bring to the boil.

Stir until the sugar has dissolved completely. Leave to cool, then divide the syrup equally between the two jars of wine. Leave until the wine has finished fermenting – about 2 weeks. Shake the jars every day during this period.

Leave the wine for a day, then siphon it into clean jars, leaving the sediment. Add 1–2 dissolved Campden tablets to each jar, cover with an airlock and leave in a cold place for 1–2 days, until the wine settles and forms a sediment. Siphon off the wine from the sediment, add finings, then filter it. Add the brandy. Bottle, cork and label the wine. Store it in a cold, dark place for at least 4–6 weeks.

MAKES ABOUT 6.8 LITRES/1½ GALLONS

– Traditional Craft Gifts –

The best craft gifts are often those based on simple and classic techniques. This chapter of ideas is intended to inspire the enthusiast who has a certain practical knack with all sorts of crafts. The ideas are simple and tasteful, and they have been chosen for their versatility. By varying the materials used you can impose your own character on the designs or adapt them to suit the taste of the recipient. The requirement is not so much for any in-depth knowledge or skill, but for time, patience and enthusiasm. An eye for colour, texture and style is always useful when making simple craft gifts. Enjoy making them, take pleasure in packing and presenting your work and the recipient is sure to be delighted with an individual gift made with love and care.

Appliqué

Appliqué can be as simple or as complicated a craft as you wish. It has a wide variety of uses, such as trimming cushion covers, towel edges, table linen and tee shirts. The chosen shape is cut out in a fabric which is usually a similar weight to the fabric of the item to be decorated but in a contrasting colour. Sometimes, a very light fabric may be applied to a heavy base, as when a self-patterned muslin, organdie or organza shape is stitched over silk or cotton.

When the chosen shape is cut, a very narrow hem should be pressed and stitched around its edge. Then the shape can be pinned in position on the fabric base. Hand or machine stitching can be used to secure the appliqué and further simple embroidery or stitching decoration may be applied to emphasize the shape or features, or to link individual appliqué shapes into a pattern.

Shapes may be cut in different colours and they may be overlapped or arranged in a wide variety of patterns. The above sample of a Victorian appliqué design was originally intended for decorating an ottoman cushion. The ivy leaves can be used on a cushion cover and it is ideal for a tablecloth and napkins. The shapes may be cut in white cotton to be sewn on a white background with the stitching in green, or green fabric shapes may be applied with matching green thread used for the stitching.

A simple leaf pattern (page 113) can be embroidered on a bought linen handkerchief or hand-hemmed fabric square to make an attractive scarf.

Patchwork

Patchwork was another popular craft in Mrs Beeton's day. This is an excellent way of turning scraps of fabric left over from dressmaking or from making curtains and other soft furnishings into presents.

The design can be a simple one, comprising squares of fabric, or an intricate pattern of two or three different shapes cut from fabrics of many colours with additional appliqué decoration.

If you are not using a purchased patchwork template, then draw a plan of the exact shape and measurements of the design, clearly showing the lines between each patch. Cut a master template in card for each shape, then cut out thin paper sections for each piece which will make up the finished article. Next cut out the fabric patches, tacking (or basting) each piece on to a piece of paper in turn. Turn a hem on to the wrong side of each patch as you tack it to the paper. When each patch is tacked on to paper, the work of assembling the whole article may be commenced.

The patches are handstitched together with tiny overcasting stitches, then the backing paper is removed. Sometimes, the patches may be sewn on a plain fabric backing to provide extra strength and prevent the fabric edges from fraying.

Hand-stitched patchwork has always been a time-consuming craft. Splendid bedspreads were produced by ladies of Mrs Beeton's day, with miles of hand-stitched quilting designs puncturing the patchwork of fabric in intricate patterns. Double-sided patchwork quilts were sometimes created on rough woollen blankets.

Modern sewing machines may be used to over-sew patchwork pieces. This greatly reduces the stitching time but it is essential to attach each patch to a suitable paper or interfacing backing

beforehand otherwise the edges of the fabric stretch and the patches pucker along the joins.

Embroidered Handkerchief

This embroidery pattern is worked between the borders of a handkerchief. The design (page 115) is simple, but effective, and very easy to work. Buy a plain white handkerchief and work the embroidery in fine white embroidery cotton. Alternatively, the design may be worked in a delicate colour, such as pale green, or use shaded green embroidery cotton for a variation in colour.

Leaf embroidery – detail.

This design for a cushion cover will inspire those who are experienced with crochet, but the same idea can be used for simple crochet-work circles, stitched together and applied to a fabric backing. The cover can be made in a variety of colours or fabric types.

The rows of raised dots should be worked first, and then the graceful branches of pointed leaves added in satin stitch. The plain round dots may be worked in bright red cotton. If working on a fine handkerchief, use fine embroidery cotton for best results.

Handkerchiefs can be made from small squares of fine cotton fabric, in either delicate or dramatic colours. For example, a bold-coloured fabric can be used with matching or contrasting colours – golden yellow on deep blue or grey on black.

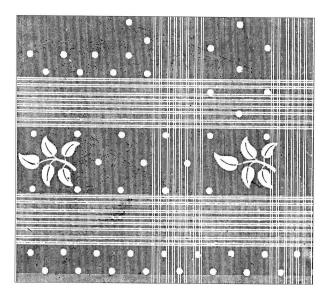

Embroidered Scarf

The pattern can also be used to embroider the corner of a square silk scarf or it can be worked at one end of a long scarf. If a sheer fabric is used, the embroidery can be worked as shadow work, using the same colour embroidery silk as the fabric and outlining the shape on the right side, then filling it in on the wrong side of the fabric.

A simple pattern of squares is the basis for these rustic cushion covers, backed and trimmed with fabric - the ideal gift for someone with smart garden furniture or a new conservatory. The pattern also can be worked in bright colours or pastel yarns for completely different effects.

Crochet Cushion Cover

This pattern can be adapted to make a round or square cushion cover. The finished crochet may be lined with a soft toning shade or a deep colour may be used. Deep-coloured satin fabric will show through the crochet to good effect. A satin-backed fabric can be used to make a matt backing for the cushion with the satin side used as a base for the crochet work. The cover shown on page 112 is made from crochet cotton (equivalent to DMC 8 thickness), using a 1.5 mm crochet hook.

Make a chain of 4 stitches, and unite it.

1st round: Work into 1 loop a double treble, make 1 chain stitch, work another double treble into the same place, make 1 chain, repeat.

2nd round: Work 3 double trebles into 1 loop, make 2 chain stitches, miss 1 loop, and repeat.

3rd round: Work 1 double crochet into the 2 chain in last round, make 7 chain, and repeat.

4th round: Into the 7 chain, work 2 double crochet, 5 double trebles, and 2 more double crochet, and repeat.

5th round: Work 1 double treble into the 1st double crochet in last round, make 9 chain, and repeat.

6th round: Into the 9 chain, work 2 double crochet, * make 4 chain, work 2 double crochet, repeat from * 3 times more, make 5 chain, work a stitch of single crochet into the 2nd of the 5, make 1 chain stitch, and repeat from the beginning of the round.

7th round: Work 1 double treble into the loop formed with the 5 chain, make 12 chain, and repeat.

8th round: Into the 12 chain, work 2 double crochet into successive loops, make 4 chain, work 1 double crochet into each of the 2 next loops, make 1 chain, work into the 6th loop 1 double crochet, 5 double trebles, and another double crochet, make 1 chain, miss 1 loop, work 2 double crochet into successive loops, make 4 chain, work 1 double crochet into each of the 2 next, make 5 chain, and repeat. This completes the circle.

To make a round cushion cover, work 1 circle for the centre larger than the others; (this can be done by repeating the 5th and 6th rounds) then sew 8 circles round the centre one, and increase the number of circles in each row until you have made it the size you wish.

To make a large crochet cover or chair back, work 120 circles and sew them together to make a cover measuring about 30 cm/12 inches long by 25 cm/10 inches wide.

Tassels may be added to decorate the corners. These are made by winding the cotton over a piece of 7.5–10 cm/3–4 inch wide cardboard. Wind the cotton around the card about 80 times. Twist 8 threads of the cotton into a cord and thread this through the cotton on the card. Cut the cotton wound on the cardboard at one end. Twist the thread together and knot the end. Bind a piece of cotton firmly around the cotton just below the twisted thread and tie it neatly to make the tassel. Overstitch the binding in a contrasting colour, if liked.

Knitted cushion cover – detail.

Knitted Cushion Cover

Thick or fine cotton may be used according to the result required and both sides of the cushion cover can be knitted or a fabric backing can be used to complement the knitted front. Each two-square pattern repeat is made up of 19 stitches.

The simple embroidery pattern may be added, if liked, when the knitting is complete, before the cover is sewn on to the backing fabric. The embroidery may be worked in cotton of the same weight to tone with the backing or in a completely different colour. The flowers are simply 5 chain stitches worked from the centre of the squares.

For double knitting wool or cotton of equivalent thickness, use 3.5 mm needles. To make a 40 cm/ 16 inch cushion cover, cast on 87 stitches.

1st row: *knit 11. Alternately 4 times, knit 2 together, throw cotton forward. Repeat from *.

2nd row: purl 1, throw cotton forward, purl 2 together, throw cotton forward, purl 2 together, throw cotton forward, purl 11. *Alternately 4 times, purl 2 together, throw cotton forward. Repeat from *. Work these two rows alternately until 12 rows are completed: this makes one block of squares.

13th row: the squares are reversed. Knit 1. *Alternately 4 times, knit 2 together, throw cotton forward, knit 11. Repeat from *. Knit 2 at end of row.

14th row: purl 2. *Alternately 4 times, purl 2 together, throw cotton forward, purl 11. Repeat from *. When a further 12 rows of pattern are completed (24 rows in all, completing the second block of squares), reverse the pattern, by working as for the 1st and 2nd rows.

The star figures are embroidered by working 5 chain stitch in the middle of each square; draw the needle underneath the knitting to the next centre of a square.

Knitted Table Centrepiece

This is a project for an experienced knitter as the pattern is worked on four needles. Distribute the stitches evenly between three needles and knit with the fourth needle. It is important to knit the first stitch on every needle in every round tightly; if these stitches are loose, they create a ladder effect in the pattern. Insert a piece of coloured thread as a row marker at the beginning of the first round of the pattern to avoid confusion. Each round is knitted: there are no purl rows.

Cast on 4 stitches, join them into a circle.

1st round: Throw the cotton forward, knit 1. Repeat 3 times.

2nd round: Entirely knitted.

3rd round: *Throw the cotton forward, knit 1. Repeat 7 times more from *.

Note: After every pattern round, knit 1 round plain, until the 21st round. For each of the following rounds, repeat the instructions seven times more to complete the circular pattern.

5th round: Throw the cotton forward, knit 2.

Note: From the 7th to the 12th round, the knitted stitches in every other round increase by 1 stitch, so that in the 12th round there are 7 stitches between those formed by throwing the cotton forward.

13th round: Throw the cotton forward, knit 2 together, knit 4, knit 2 together.

15th round: Throw the cotton forward, knit 1, throw the cotton forward, knit 2 together, knit 2, knit 2 together.

17th round: Throw the cotton forward, knit 3, throw the cotton forward, knit 2 together, knit 2 together.

19th round: Throw the cotton forward, knit 5, throw the cotton forward, knit 2 together.

21st round: Knit 1, throw the cotton forward, knit 5, throw the cotton forward, knit 2.

22nd round: Knit 2, knit 2 together, knit 1, knit 2 together, knit 3.

23rd round: Knit 2, throw the cotton forward, knit 3, throw the cotton forward, knit 3.

24th round: Knit 3, knit 2 together, knit 5.

25th round: Knit 3, throw the cotton forward, knit 2 together, throw the cotton forward, knit 4.

26th round: Entirely knitted.

27th round: Throw the cotton forward, knit 9, throw the cotton forward, knit 1.

28th round: Entirely knitted.

29th round: Knit 1, throw the cotton forward, knit 9, throw the cotton forward, knit 2.

30th round: Entirely knitted.

31st round: Knit 2, throw the cotton forward, knit 9, throw the cotton forward, knit 3.

32nd round: Entirely knitted.

33rd round: Knit 3, throw the cotton forward, knit 9, throw the cotton forward, knit 4.

34th round: Knit 4, knit 2 together, knit 5, knit 2 together, knit 5.

35th round: Knit 4, throw the cotton forward, knit 7, throw the cotton forward, knit 5.

36th round: Knit 5, knit 2 together, knit 3, knit 2 together, knit 6.

37th round: Throw the cotton forward, knit 5 three times, throw the cotton forward, knit 1.

38th round: Knit 7, knit 2 together, knit 1, knit 2 together , knit 8.

39th round: Knit 1, throw the cotton forward, knit 6, throw the cotton forward, knit 3, throw the cotton forward, knit 6, throw the cotton forward, knit 2.

40th round: Knit 9, knit 3 together, knit 10.

41st round: Knit 2, throw the cotton forward, knit 15, throw the cotton forward, knit 3.

42nd round: Knit 3, knit 2 together, knit 11, knit 2 together, knit 4.

43rd round: Knit 3, throw the cotton forward, knit 13, throw the cotton forward, knit 4.

44th round: Knit 4, knit 2 together, knit 9, knit 2 together, knit 5.

Border: Cast on 5 stitches and knit the

1st row: slip 1, throw the cotton forward, knit 2 together, throw the cotton forward, knit 2.

2nd row: Slip 1, knit the rest. Repeat this row after every pattern row.

3rd row: Slip 1, throw the cotton forward, knit 2 together, throw the cotton forward, knit 2 together, throw the cotton forward , knit 1.

5th row: Slip 1, throw the cotton forward, knit 2 together, throw the cotton forward, knit 2 together, throw the cotton forward, knit 2.

7th row: Slip 1, throw the cotton forward, knit 2 together, throw the cotton forward, knit 2 together, throw the cotton forward, knit 2 together, throw the cotton forward, knit 1.

9th row: Slip 1, throw the cotton forward, knit 2 together, throw the cotton forward, knit 2 together, throw the cotton forward, knit 2 together, throw the cotton forward, knit 2.

11th row: Slip 1, throw the cotton forward, knit 2 together, throw the cotton forward, knit 2 together, throw the cotton forward, knit 2 together, throw the cotton forward, knit 2 together, knit 1.

13th row: Slip 1, throw the cotton forward, knit 2 together, throw the cotton forward, knit 2 together, throw the cotton forward, knit 2 together, throw the cotton forward, knit 2 together, throw the cotton forward, knit 2.

15th row: Cast off 8 stitches, throw the cotton forward, knit 2 together, throw the cotton forward, knit 1.

16th row: Entirely knitted.

Continue, beginning again at the 1st row, knitting a sufficient length to trim the centrepiece.

Covered Coat Hangers

Inexpensive and easy to make, covered coat hangers make an attractive gift. Scraps of cotton dressmaking fabric can be used as can lightweight curtain materials. Satin or silk are both suitable and lace fabrics look most attractive over a plain cotton cover. Velvet makes a useful non-slip cover on which to hang lightweight silk blouses.

Most of the covered hangers available in the shops tend to be too small to usefully support the shoulders of blouses and dresses. Select a hanger and pad by binding it with old tights or stockings, foam or wadding. Tights are ideal as they are inexpensive and they can be wound around the hanger, then stitched in place. When the hanger is well padded, lay it on a piece of paper and draw a pattern from which to cut the fabric, allowing enough to curve over the top of the padding plus 1 cm/ ½ inch all around for a seam. Draw the pattern a short way up the curve of the hook. Pin the pattern to a double thickness of fabric, placed right sides together, and cut it out.

Stitch the fabric together, making a 1 cm/½ inch seam, from one end across the top to the hook, then from the other side of the hook along to the other end. Leave the bottom open so that the cover can be placed over the hanger. Turn the fabric so that the right side is out and press the seam open flat. If the top is curved, make short snips into the seam to prevent it from pulling. Turn back and handstitch a single hem along the cut edge through which the hook will be inserted. Place the cover over the hanger and handstitch a neat seam along the bottom.

Neaten the fabric around the base of the hook by gathering it tightly and sewing on a length of complementary ribbon. Leave enough ribbon to tie a bow around the base of the hook.

Drawstring Toilet Bag or Make-up Bag

A small drawstring bag can be made for holding make up or for other toiletries. Select a washable fabric with lining in a plain colour to complement a patterned exterior. Wash and press both the outer fabric and lining before making the bag to ensure that it will not shrink or fade badly when washed after some use. Satin or a heavy, patterned curtain fabric are both suitable for toilet bags, when lined with towelling. Buy suitable cord to match the fabric for the drawstring.

For a large toilet bag, allow enough fabric to cut two oblongs measuring about 30 × 23 cm/12 × 9 inches. A smaller bag (for make-up) can be made to measure about 20 × 15 cm/8 × 6 inches. Cut two oblongs of outer fabric and two oblongs of lining.

Make a mark 5 cm/2 inches down from the top on each side of the larger oblongs. If making the smaller bag make the marks about 3.5 cm/1½ inches down the sides. Place the outer oblongs of fabric right sides together and sew down the sides as far as the mark making a 1 cm/½ in seam on both sides. Leave a gap of 2 cm/¾ inch unstitched on each side, then continue sewing the seam to 1 cm/½ inch from the bottom of the fabric and across the bottom of the bag. The gap is for the drawstring. Sew the lining in exactly the same way, right sides together, and leave the base open. Press the seams flat, folding the fabric back neatly along the gap. Finish off the edges of the fabric seam inside the gap and handstitch the seam in place to prevent it from pulling out when the bag is in use.

Fit the lining over the outside of the outer fabric, with right sides of the fabric together and the top edges matching. Stitch a 1 cm/½ in hem around the top, then turn the lining inside the bag and press the top edge neatly. Stitch the bottom of the lining to complete the inner bag.

Use tailors' chalk and a ruler to draw straight lines between the top and bottom of the gaps across both sides of the bag. Stitch the lining and outer fabric together along these lines on both sides of the bag to make a channel in which to insert the

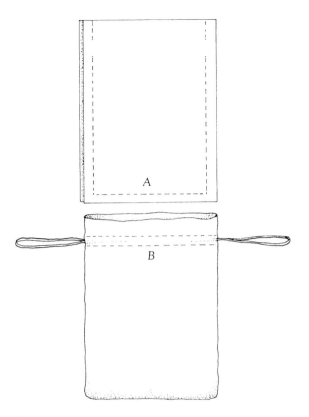

A Leave this edge open in lining.
B Stitch channel on outside of finished bag, through outer fabric and lining.

Lavender Bags and Pouches

Pick the lavender when it is in the first beauty of bloom, tie it in bunches and hang it to dry in a warm, dry place away from direct sunlight. When dry the fragrant flowers may be rubbed off the stalks and used to fill small bags or pouches of fine fabric.

The fabric must be fine to allow the fragrance of the herb to penetrate it. Muslin, cheesecloth, silk or a closely woven lace fabric may be used. Very plain fabrics may be covered with decorative lace if wished. Gathered lace, ribbon or neat piping may be applied to the edge of the lavender bags.

To make a simple bag, cut two 10 cm/4 inch squares of fabric. Pin the squares together with the right sides of the fabric inside. Sew a narrow seam all around the edge, leaving a gap of about 5 cm/ 2 inches or slightly less on one side. Trim the points off the corners of the fabric, then turn the bag inside out so that the raw edges are enclosed. Fill the bag with lavender, then stitch up the opening. Use small stitches to attach lace around the edge of the bag. Add a ribbon loop and bow so that the fragrant sachet may be hung on the hook of a coat hanger.

A small lavender pouch may be made by cutting a slightly larger square of fabric – about 15 cm/ 6 inches along each side. Fold the raw edges of the fabric over twice into a very narrow hem and press them with a hot iron. Then sew them neatly with tiny stitches. Attach a lace edge all around the fabric. Cut a length of very narrow baby ribbon. Pile a small mound of lavender flowers in the middle of the fabric, then gather it up and tie the lavender in securely with the ribbon. Leave the corners of the pouch hanging free. Attach a loop and bow of ribbon, tying it firmly above the lavender filling.

drawstring. Brush off the tailors' chalk. If liked, lace or gathered ribbon trimming can be neatly hand-stitched over the channel to conceal the stitching, but take care not to sew up the channel.

Measure two lengths of cord for drawstrings, long enough to fit across the width of the bag and to make ties. A rouleau loop can be made from either the lining or the outer fabric instead of cutting cord drawstrings: cut a narrow strip of fabric, fold it in half and sew it together across one end and down the side. Then use a knitting needle to turn the strip inside out and handstitch the open end. Press the loop flat. Thread the drawstrings through the channels using a small safety pin as a guide.

The ends of the drawstrings may be sewn or tied together and finished off with a knot or by adding a decorative feature, such as matching tassels. Large beads may be knotted on the ends of the draw-strings.

Refreshing Foot Bath

Mix 15 g/½ oz each of dried mint and sage with 100 g/ 4 oz lightly crushed juniper berries and 100 g/4 oz dried rosemary. Put the mixture into an attractive jar with an airtight lid. The mixture may be used as an infusion for a foot bath or it can be tied in small squares of muslin and added to a large bath. Small muslin pouches of mixture can be gathered up with cotton, then tied with baby ribbon and packed in a jar – rather like commercial bouquets garnis. With the right choice of ribbon and jar, the bath pouches are ideal for men as well as women.

Preserved Flower Gifts

Pressing Flowers

Pick perfect blooms on a fine day. Avoid flowers that have been attacked by insects. Lay the flowers on a piece of blotting paper, arranging the petals carefully and flattening them into a neat shape without any folds. Place a second piece of blotting paper on top. Then sandwich the double blotting paper between two sheets of ordinary white cartridge paper and put the flowers in a press. Alternatively, place them between two books and leave until dry.

A small flower press may be made from plywood, cut to a suitable size. Drill a hole in each corner and fit four bolts through the holes, then apply thumb-screws to secure the press. Several layers of flowers may be flattened in the press but they must be divided by pieces of corrugated cardboard. Flowers with thick centres may be protected by covering with a piece of cardboard with the centre cut out, allowing the petals to be pressed but preventing the centre of the bloom from being squashed.

Gift Ideas

* Decorate plain cardboard boxes by gluing an arrangement of pressed flowers on top. If liked,

the top of the box may be varnished with a suitable paper varnish once the glue has dried. Trim the box with ribbon.

* Glue small pressed flowers to the corners of note paper. They make an attractive alternative to 'thank you' cards.

* When presenting an edible gift, such as a pot of pâté, make a large tag with serving instructions and decorate it with pressed flowers.

* Trim the front of a plain notebook with pressed flowers. Tie a small bow of very fine ribbon through the middle of the book and around the spine. This idea lends itself to a variety of gifts. Divide a notebook into sections (Soups and Starters; Fish Dishes; Meat and Poultry; Vegetables and Vegetarian Dishes; Desserts; Cakes and Biscuits), write in a few of your favourite recipes and you have a gift the recipient will treasure. A visitors' book or a notebook for recording details of dinner party menus will be equally acceptable, while the keen golfer might welcome a book for jotting down scores.

* Compile a notebook of herbs, for jotting down herb ideas and recipes. Decorate the pages with sprigs of pressed herbs stuck in the corners, with their names written neatly underneath. Write in a few of your favourite herb growing notes, recipes or tips and leave plenty of room for the recipient to add his or her ideas as they discover different ways of using the plants.

* Use pressed flowers to make greetings cards (page 20). Wrap four to six cards together in cellophane, securing it neatly underneath the cards with small pieces of adhesive tape. Tie fine ribbon around the pack of cards.

* Decorate an old plain tray with pressed flowers. A tatty, old-fashioned tin tray can be made to look quite splendid when sprayed with colour or with gold or bronze paint or a wooden tray can be thoroughly sanded to remove the remnants of varnish and any stains. Take care when gluing the flowers in place, making a small arrangement on each corner of the tray or curving across the middle. When the glue has dried completely, carefully apply a coat of clear polyurethane varnish, working gently over each of the flowers first, then over the rest of the tray. Apply another coat or two of varnish once the first application has dried.

Dried Flower Gifts

Everlasting flowers are easy to grow and dry. The flowers should be picked as soon as they open and before they reach their prime. Pick the flowers on a dry day and hang them upside down in a warm room for about 2 weeks, or until they are dry. Even if you do not grow your own flowers it can still be more economical to buy the fresh flowers from a florist and to dry them at home rather than buying ready dried flowers.

* Fill small or large baskets with dried flowers and grasses. Add a decorative bow of unravelled twisted paper to a basket handle.

* An old vegetable tureen which has lost its lid makes an ideal container for dried flowers.

* A hanging basket of dried flowers can be made using a basket in a macramé hanging rope. Alternatively, weave partially unravelled twisted paper between the wires of an outdoor hanging basket. Weave occasional groups of dried flowers around the outside of the basket; fill the top with flowers and grasses. Weave paper or fabric ribbon through the hanging chains and tie bows at the bases of the chains.

* Make a wreath of dried flowers. Use a polystyrene ring base and trim the flower stalks before fitting them into the ring. Fill the ring with grasses and add ribbon loops with short lengths of floristry wire twisted around their bases to fill the gaps. A cane wreath base may be used but it can be difficult to secure dried flowers between the cane. Tie small bunches of dried flowers with fine floristry wire, leaving enough wire to twist around the cane, and cover the wire binding with narrow ribbon, tying it in a bow. Fix the bunches of flowers and ribbon on the cane, leaving the stalks showing and allowing ribbon tails to drape from the bows. Dried spices, such as cinnamon sticks or star anise are interesting additions to fill spaces between small bunches of dried flowers.

* Make a colourful and aromatic pot pourri by mixing dried bay leaves, dried rosemary sprigs and cinnamon bark (second-grade cinnamon usually available from ethnic supermarkets, sold as chunks of bark rather than fine rolled sticks). Add whole star anise if available. Pare the rind off oranges and allow it to dry in twisting strips, then add these to the pot pourri. Sprinkle a little pot pourri oil over the mixture, then add a couple of handfuls of dried flower heads and dried poppy seed heads. This is a good way of using broken dried flowers and stray blossoms that are too short to be fixed into an arrangement. Mix well and tie the mixture in a polythene bag, adding a ribbon bow and a gift tag.

Decorated Eggs

Painted eggs are a fun alternative to chocolate eggs as an Easter present. The eggs can be painted or decorated in all sorts of ways, according to your artistic interests and ability. Hand-painted designs can be beautiful, but if your talents lie in other directions, adopt a different approach and spray the eggs gold or silver, then add a simple spot or dot pattern, or glue some dried flowers on the eggs. The first stage is to blow the eggs and prepare the shells. Wash and dry an egg. Have a basin ready for the raw egg. Use a sharp needle to prick a hole in both ends of the egg. Use a gentle screwing action to make and enlarge the holes, making sure that the membrane inside is pierced. Hold the egg over the basin and blow hard into one hole, until all of the egg has emerged through the bottom hole. Wash the shell well under hot water, stoppering the bottom hole with a finger and running in water through the top hole, then shaking the shell well so that the water effectively cleans the inside. Finally blow the egg again to remove the water. Rinse the shell several times, blow it out well and leave to dry.

Spray-paint the eggs with a base coat of spray colour and leave it to dry before brushing on a design. Enamel paints can be used to make an attractive, permanent pattern. Alternatively, a small stencil or pattern may be placed on the egg and spray paint applied in a second colour. A base coat of gold paint decorated with rich enamel colours can look very smart.

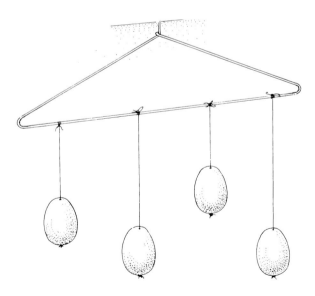

Hang the eggs on pieces of thread from a coat hanger, placing the hook of the hanger securely over a ledge or inside a deep cake tin, weighted down with a heavy object. Tie the eggs at different lengths so that they do not touch each other, then spray them with a base coat of paint.

Dried or pressed flowers may be glued on the eggs. Sequins or beads can also be glued on the shells in attractive patterns.

Fine baby ribbon may be threaded through the egg using a long darning needle. Knot the ribbon or tie a bow in it underneath the egg, then stitch the top in a loop by which to hang the egg. If you cannot thread the ribbon through, simply glue a loop of ribbon on the top of the egg.

Play-dough Decorations

Salt dough, or play dough, can be used to make long-lasting decorations. It is particularly popular for making Christmas decorations to hang on the tree. You can make personalized shapes for your friends (perhaps using their initials), create tiny decorations to hang on parcels or fill a Christmas stocking, or even mould small items to furnish a doll's house or a play shop.

The shapes can be as simple as the designer pleases. A plain ring twisted and baked to a toasty-brown, dangling from a bright red ribbon looks just as enchanting as a complicated plait or a flower with multi-coloured petals. If you wish to make cut-out shapes and do not have suitable biscuit cutters, draw around shapes from cards or books and make card templates.

The baked shapes may be painted and allowed to dry, then preserved with several coats of varnish. Allow each coat to dry before applying the next.

When encouraging children to make gifts, do not allow them to get so carried away with the excitement of the craft that they expect to be able to eat the decorations after all. The dough is unbearably salty and baked to an unpalatable degree of hardness to make it long-lasting and prevent the growth of mould.

THE BASIC DOUGH

450 g/1 lb plain flour
175 g/ 6 oz salt
10 ml/2 tsp glycerine
water (see method)
food colourings (optional)

GLAZE (OPTIONAL)
1 egg yolk
15 ml/1 tbsp milk

Mix the flour, salt and glycerine in a bowl. Pour on enough water to make a fairly stiff dough. Shape the dough into a ball and put it in a plastic bag. Leave it in the refrigerator for several hours, or overnight.

The next day, knead the dough by hand, or in a food processor until smooth. If you want to colour the dough, this is the time to do it. Tear off small pieces of the dough, put them into bowls and sprinkle on one or two drops of food colouring. Knead thoroughly. If the colour is too intense, add more plain dough and knead again.

Roll out the dough on a lightly floured board to an even thickness of about 6 mm/$\frac{3}{16}$ inch. Do not make tree decorations too thick or they will hang heavily on the branches. Cut out the shapes you require, or mould the dough to make fruit, 'mince pies' and so on.

To make plaits, one of the traditional salt-dough decorations, cut three strips about 2 cm/$\frac{3}{4}$ inch wide. Roll the strips to make sausage shapes. Press one end of each of the strips together and plait them in the usual way. Cut off the dough at the ends, shape the plait into a circle and press the joined ends together. Cut out bow or leaf shapes to cover the join, or cover it with a neat ribbon after baking.

Use a toothpick to press a hole into solid shapes, for the hanging ribbon. Mark on any texture details, such as leaf veins.

Brush uncoloured dough with a glaze of beaten egg and milk and place the shapes well apart on a baking sheet. Leave them in a warm room for at least 24 hours so that they dry thoroughly before baking.

Set the oven at 160°C/325°F/gas 3. Bake the dough for 1–1$\frac{1}{2}$ hours or until the shapes are completely dry. Remove them from the oven and leave them to cool.

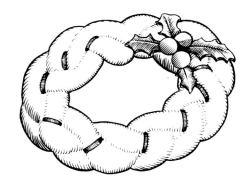

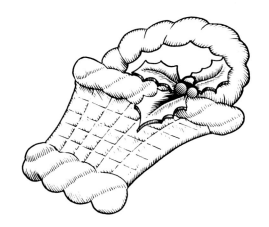

Ways to use Play-dough Shapes

* If you want to paint the dough when it is baked, do not glaze it with egg and milk before baking. This will give it a matt, fairly pale finish.

* Make gingerbread men shapes, and stand them, hands linked, around an indoor flower pot which is to be used for a table-top Christmas tree or decoration. Attach the play-dough men to the pot with small dabs of blue tacky clay.

* Make the play-dough into twisted candle shapes to fit small Christmas tree holders. You can colour the candles red, the flames orange – or not, as you wish. They will symbolize the light in a safe, unusual and decorative way.

* Make a nativity scene of play-dough figures and stand them in a group on a board covered with hay or straw.

* Make simple fruit shapes such as apples and pears and pile them in a pottery dish.

* Take a design tip from Finland. Make a large play-dough heart and hang it on a red ribbon. Hearts can be made and decorated by gluing on dried flowers when the dough is baked, varnished and dried.

* Make and bake initials, then paint and varnish them. Decorate with dried flowers and a bow of ribbon when dry.

* Cut out a square, oblong, oval or round greetings plaque from the rolled-out dough and place it on the baking sheet. Cake decorating tools are ideal for making patterns in the dough or use aspic cutters to make pattern impressions around the edge of the dough. Stamp out tiny flowers, hearts or other shapes and stick them around the edge of the plaque with a little water. Add leaves or other decorative shapes. Make a hole in the top of the plaque for a hanging ribbon. Glaze the middle of the dough but leave the flowers, or any decorative shapes which can be painted, uncoloured. Paint the plaque and write a message in the middle. Glaze it with varnish, if you like, then add a ribbon bow at the top.

* Brooches and refrigerator magnets can all be made from small decorative dough models.

* Small, colourful dough shapes can be suspended from wire to make a simple mobile. Bind two lengths of floristry wire into a cross and spray them gold, if liked. Use fine, transparent, nylon thread to hang a small dough model from the end of each piece of wire. Tie a length of nylon thread from the middle of the cross and use it to hang the mobile.

Growing Plants

Plants make acceptable gifts on any occasion for both men and women. Children love to receive a pot of fast-growing flowers. Making up a large pot or planter of bulbs, herbs, flowering plants or evergreens is an excellent way of putting together an individual gift for someone special. Instead of a random selection of plants, take care when choosing them, matching plants that thrive in similar conditions (sun or shade, dry or moist conditions) and coordinating colours, foliage and height. If you are planting a large outdoor pot, you may like to include an evergreen with spring or summer flowering plants or bulbs so that the pot looks lively throughout the year. Always try to pot the plants at least a few days before giving the present, so that they are settled and look as though they belong. Finish the pot with an attractive bow of ribbon. Here are a few ideas for growing gifts.

* A large pot of basil is ideal for the cook with a conservatory or a sunny patio. If you do not have time to plant and grow seeds, buy two or three herb plants from the supermarket (sold ready for cooking) as they grow really well.

* A large planter of mixed herbs, or a special tiered pot for growing herbs, can be potted with several different plants. Pots of mixed plants are not suitable for herbs that are used in large quantities, such as basil or parsley, but they are useful for small bushes of rosemary, thyme, savory and tarragon.

* An outdoor climbing plant can be potted in a large tub with a length of trellis or a wig-wam arrangement of bean poles. Flower plants, such as sweet peas, look good planted in this way and they brighten up a small patio.

* An evergreen pot or hanging basket makes an acceptable gift. Select plants that provide variation in leaf shape and colour, including trailing plants as well as an upward-growing evergreen.

* A potted shrub is often a good choice of gift, particularly for anyone moving into a new home. Make sure there is plenty of room for the shrub to grow and that the pot is large enough to retain ample moisture otherwise the soil around the shrub will quickly dry out in warm weather.

* Buy a large mortar and pestle, then find a suitable plastic carton to fit the mortar. Plant a herb, such as coriander, in the carton and cover the outside with colourful cellophane paper, then stand it in the mortar.

* Present a small pot of camomile in a china mug.

* Fill a window box with a pair of scented herbs, such as trailing thyme and basil. They will grow well in a sunny position outside during the summer.

* Keen cooks will appreciate a collection of different mint plants. There are many different varieties, including variegated plants and some with distinctly different flavours. As well as common mint, include cologne mint (super for scenting summer drinks and fruit cups), apple mint and pineapple mint. Leave the mints in their separate pots and pack them in a polythene-lined basket, surrounding them with crumpled or shredded green tissue. Remind the recipient that the different mints should be planted separately as some of the very strong plants will quickly choke the more delicate varieties, such as the variegated mint. The same idea can be used for sage or thyme, as there are several types of both herbs.

-Index-